DK TRAVEL GUIDES

RUSSIAN
PHRASE BOOK

D0493950

A Dorling Kindersley Book

Dorling **DK** Kindersley

LONDON, NEW YORK, MUNICH,
MELBOURNE, AND DELHI

www.dk.com

Compiled by Lexus Ltd with Geoffrey and Ekaterina Smith
Printed and bound in Italy by Printer Trento Srl.

First published in Great Britain in 1998
by Dorling Kindersley Limited
80 Strand, London WC2R ORL

Reprinted with corrections 2000
2 4 6 8 10 9 7 5 3

Dorling Kindersley books can be purchased in bulk quantities at
discounted prices for use in promotions or as premiums. We are
also able to offer special editions and personalized jackets, corporate
imprints, and excerpts from all of our books, tailored specifically to
meet your own needs. To find out more, please contact: Special Sales,
Dorling Kindersley Limited, 80 Strand, London WC2R ORL;
Tel. 020 7010 3000.

A CIP catalogue record is available from the British Library.

ISBN 0 7513 1088 3

Picture Credits

Jacket: all images special photography Demetrio Carrasco,
Andy Crawford and John Heseltine.

CONTENTS

PREFACE

This *Dorling Kindersley Travel Guides Phrase Book* has been compiled by experts to meet the general needs of tourists and business travellers. Arranged under headings such as Hotels, Driving and so forth, the ample selection of useful words and phrases is supported by a 2,000-line mini-dictionary. There is also an extensive menu guide listing approximately 300 dishes or methods of cooking and presentation.

Typical replies to questions you may ask during your journey, and the signs or instructions you may see or hear, are shown in tinted boxes. In the main text, the pronunciation of Russian words and phrases is imitated in English sound syllables. There is a comprehensive guide to Russian pronunciation at the beginning of the book.

Dorling Kindersley Travel Guides are recognised as the world's best travel guides. Each title features specially commissioned colour photographs, cutaways of major buildings, 3-D aerial views and detailed maps, plus information on sights, events, hotels, restaurants, shopping and entertainment.

PRONUNCIATION

When reading the imitated pronunciation, stress the part that is underlined. Pronounce each syllable as if it formed part of an English word, and you will be understood sufficiently well. Remember the points below, and your pronunciation will be even closer to the correct Russian:

a	as in 'alimony'
ay	as in 'may'
e	as in 'egg'
I	as in 'die'
i	as in 'lid'
kh	as a guttural 'ch' in the Scottish pronunciation of 'loch'
o	as in 'rob'
oy	as in 'boy'
ye	as in 'yet'
zh	as 's' in 'leisure' only harder
'	no sound of its own but softens the preceding consonant and adds a slight *y* sound, eg *n'* would sound *ny* as in 'canyon'.

The mini-dictionary provides the Russian translations in the form of the imitated pronunciation so that you can read the words without reference to the Russian alphabet. In the phrases, the abbreviations *(m)* and *(f)* indicate the forms to be used by a male or female speaker respectively.

Over the page is a further guide to Russian pronunciation, alongside the Russian (Cyrillic) alphabet.

THE RUSSIAN (CYRILLIC) ALPHABET

letter		pronunciation	letter		pronunciation
А	a	*(a)* as in 'alimony'	Т	т	*(t)* as in 'toffee'
Б	б	*(b)* as in 'bed'	У	у	*(oo)* as in 'boot'
В	в	*(v)* as in 'vet'	Ф	ф	*(f)* as in 'fellow'
Г	г	*(g)* as in 'get'	Х	х	*(kh)* as in 'ch' in the Scottish 'loch'
Д	д	*(d)* as in 'debt'			
Е	е	*(ye)* as in 'yet'	Ц	ц	*(ts)* as in 'let's'
Ё	ё	*(yo)* as in 'yonder'	Ч	ч	*(ch)* as in 'chair'
Ж	ж	*(zh)* as in 'leisure', only rather harder	Ш	ш	*(sh)* as in 'shovel'
З	з	*(z)* as in 'zither'	Щ	щ	*(shsh)* as above but with a slight roll, as in 'fresh sheet'
И	и	*(ee)* as in 'see'	Ъ	ъ	hard sign – no sound but use very slight pause before next letter
Й	й	*(y)* as in 'boy'			
К	к	*(k)* as in 'king'			
Л	л	*(l)* as in 'loot'	Ы	ы	*(i)* approximately as in 'lid'
М	м	*(m)* as in 'match'			
Н	н	*(n)* as in 'never'	Ь	ь	soft sign – no sound but softens preceding consonant
О	о	*(o)* as in 'rob'			
П	п	*(p)* as in 'pea'	Э	э	*(e)* as in 'egg'
Р	р	*(r)* as in 'rat-a-tat'	Ю	ю	*(you)* as in 'youth'
С	с	*(s)* as in 'lass'	Я	я	*(ya)* as in 'yak'

USEFUL EVERYDAY PHRASES

Yes/no
Да/нет
da/nyet

Thank you
Спасибо
spas<u>ee</u>ba

No, thank you
Нет, спасибо
nyet, spas<u>ee</u>ba

Please
Пожалуйста
pazh<u>a</u>lsta

I don't understand
Я не понимаю
ya nye pan<u>ee</u>ma-yoo

Do you speak English?
Вы говорите по-английски?
vi gavar<u>ee</u>t-ye pa-angl<u>ee</u>skee

I can't speak Russian
Я не говорю по-русски
ya nye gavar<u>yoo</u> pa-r<u>oo</u>skee

I don't know
Я не знаю
ya nye zn<u>a</u>-yoo

Please speak more slowly
Пожалуйста, говорите медленнее
pazh<u>a</u>lsta, gavar<u>ee</u>t-ye m<u>y</u>edlyenye-ye

Please write it down for me
Пожалуйста, напишите это для меня
pazhalsta, napeesheet-ye eta dlya myenya

My name is …
Меня зовут ...
myenya zavoot

How do you do, pleased to meet you
Здравствуйте, очень приятно
zdrastvooyt-ye, ochen' pree-yatna

Good morning
Доброе утро
dobra-ye ootra

Good afternoon
Добрый день
dobri dyen'

Good evening
Добрый вечер
dobri vyechyer

Good night (*when going to bed*)
Спокойной ночи
spakoynay nochee

Good night (*leaving group early*)
Счастливо
shasleeva

Goodbye
До свидания
da sveedaneeya

How are you?
Как дела?
kak dyela

Excuse me, please
Извините, пожалуйста
eezveeneet-ye, pazhalsta

Sorry!
Простите!
prasteet-ye

I'm really sorry
Я очень сожалею
ya ochen' sazhilyeyoo

Can you help me?
Вы можете мне помочь?
vi mozhet-ye mnye pamoch'

Can you tell me …?
Скажите, пожалуйста ...?
skazheet-ye, pazhalsta

Can I have …?
Можно ...?
mozhna

I would like …
Я хотел (*m*)/хотела (*f*) бы ...
ya khatyel/khatyela bi

Is there … here?
Здесь есть ...?
zdyes' yest'

Where can I get …?
Где можно найти ...?
Gdye mozhna nItee

How much is it?
Сколько это стоит?
skol'ka eta sto-eet

What time is it?
Который час?
katori chas

I must go now
Мне пора идти
mnye para eetee

I've lost my way
Я заблудился (m)/заблудилась (f)
ya zabloodeelsa/zabloodeelas'

I've lost my passport/credit cards
Я потерял (m)/потеряла (f) паспорт/дорожные чеки/
кредитные карточки
ya potyeryal/potyeryala pasport/kryedeetniye kartachkee

Cheers!
Ваше здоровье!
vashe zdarov'ye

Do you take credit cards?
Вы принимаете кредитные карточки?
vi preeneema-yet-ye kryedeetniye kartachkee

Where is the toilet?
Где туалет?
gdye too-alyet

Go away!
Уходите!
ookhadeet-ye

Where is the British/US embassy?
Где находится британское/американское посольство?
gdye nakhodeetsa breetanskaye/amyereekanskaye pasol'stovo

Are there facilities for the disabled?
Здесь есть удобства для инвалидов?
Zdes' yest' udopstva dlya eenvaleedaf

Excellent!
Отлично!
atleechna

THINGS YOU'LL HEAR

astarozhna!	Look out!
ay!	Hey!
da sveedaneeya	Goodbye
eezveeneet-ye	Excuse me
kak dyela?	How are you?
kharasho, spaseeba, a u vas?	Fine, thank you – and you?
ooveedeemsa	See you later
pazhalsta	You're welcome
pravda?	Is that so?
praveel'na	That's right
shto, prasteet-ye?	Pardon?
spaseeba	Thanks
vot, pazhalsta	Here you are
ya nye paneema-yoo	I don't understand
ya nye zna-yoo	I don't know
zdrastvooyt-ye, ochen' preeyatna	How do you do, nice to meet you

THINGS YOU'LL SEE

вода для питья	*vada dlya peet'ya*	drinking water
вход	*fkhot*	way in/entrance
вход воспрещён	*fkhot vaspryeshshyon*	no admittance
входите	*fkhadeet-ye*	come straight in
вход свободный	*fkhot svabodni*	admission free
выход	*vikhat*	way out/exit
Ж/женский туалет	*zhenskee too-alyet*	women
заказано	*zakazana*	reserved
закрыто	*zakrita*	closed
занято	*zanyata*	engaged
запасной выход	*zapasnoy vikhot*	emergency exit
Интурист	*eentooreest*	Intourist
касса	*kasa*	till
к себе	*ksyeb-ye*	pull
лифт	*leeft*	lift
М		underground; men
мужской туалет	*mooshskoy tooalyet*	men
осторожно, окрашено	*astarozhna, akrashyena*	caution, wet paint
открыто	*atkrita*	open
от себя	*atsyebya*	push
пожарный выход	*pazharni vikhat*	fire exit
посторонним вход воспрещён	*pastaroneem fkhot vaspryeshshon*	private/no admittance
рынок	*rinak*	market
соблюдайте тишину	*sablyoodalt-ye teesheenoo*	silence/quiet
туалеты	*too-alyeti*	toilets
часы работы	*chasi raboti*	opening times

DAYS, MONTHS, SEASONS

Sunday	воскресенье	*vaskryesyen'ye*
Monday	понедельник	*panyedyel'neek*
Tuesday	вторник	*ftorneek*
Wednesday	среда	*sryeda*
Thursday	четверг	*chyetvyerk*
Friday	пятница	*pyatneetsa*
Saturday	суббота	*soobota*

January	январь	*yeenvar'*
February	февраль	*fyevral'*
March	март	*mart*
April	апрель	*apryel'*
May	май	*mI*
June	июнь	*ee-yoon'*
July	июль	*ee-yool'*
August	август	*avgoost*
September	сентябрь	*syentyabr'*
October	октябрь	*aktyabr'*
November	ноябрь	*na-yabr'*
December	декабрь	*dyekabr'*

Spring	весна	*vyesna*
Summer	лето	*lyeta*
Autumn	осень	*osyen'*
Winter	зима	*zeema*

Christmas	Рождество	*razhdyestvo*
Christmas Eve	Сочельник	*sachyel'neek*
New Year	Новый год	*novi god*
New Year's Eve	Новогодняя ночь	*navagodnya-ya noch'*

NUMBERS

0 ноль *nol'*
1 один/одна/одно *adeen/adna/adno*
2 два/две *dva/dvye*
3 три *tree*
4 четыре *chyetir-ye*

5 пять *pyat'*
6 шесть *shest'*
7 семь *syem'*
8 восемь *vosyem'*
9 девять *dyevyat'*

10 десять *dyesyat'*
11 одиннадцать *adeenatsat'*
12 двенадцать *dvyenatsat'*
13 тринадцать *treenatsat'*
14 четырнадцать *chyetirnatsat'*
15 пятнадцать *pyatnatsat'*
16 шестнадцать *shesnatsat'*
17 семнадцать *syemnatsat'*
18 восемнадцать *vasyemnatsat'*
19 девятнадцать *dyevyatnatsat'*
20 двадцать *dvatsat'*
21 двадцать один *dvatsat' adeen*
22 двадцать два *dvatsat' dva*
30 тридцать *treetsat'*
31 тридцать один *treetsat' adeen*
32 тридцать два *treetsat' dva*
40 сорок *sorak*
50 пятьдесят *pyadyesyat*
60 шестьдесят *shesdyesyat*
70 семьдесят *syem'dyesyat*
80 восемьдесят *vosyem'dyesyat*
90 девяносто *dyevyanosta*
100 сто *sto*
110 сто десять *sto dyesyat'*
200 двести *dvyestee*
300 триста *treesta*

15

400	четыреста	*chyetiryesta*
500	пятьсот	*pyat'sot*
600	шестьсот	*shesot*
700	семьсот	*syem'sot*
800	восемьсот	*vasyem'sot*
900	девятьсот	*dyevyat'sot*
1,000	тысяча	*tisyacha*
10,000	десять тысяч	*dyesyat' tisyach*
20,000	двадцать тысяч	*dvatsat' tisyach*
100,000	сто тысяч	*sto tisyach*
1,000,000	миллион	*meelee-on*

ORDINAL NUMBERS

1st	первое	*pyerva-ye*
2nd	второе	*ftaro-ye*
3rd	третье	*tryet'ye*
4th	четвёртое	*chyetvyorta-ye*
5th	пятое	*pyata-ye*
6th	шестое	*shesto-ye*
7th	седьмое	*cyed'mo-ye*
8th	восьмое	*vas'mo-ye*
9th	девятое	*dyevyata-ye*
10th	десятое	*dyesyata-ye*
11th	одиннадцатое	*adeenatsata-ye*
12th	двенадцатое	*dvyenatsata-ye*
13th	тринадцатое	*treenatsata-ye*
14th	четырнадцатое	*chyetirnatsata-ye*
15th	пятнадцатое	*pyatnatsata-ye*
16th	шестнадцатое	*shesnatsata-ye*
17th	семнадцатое	*syemnatsata-ye*
18th	восемнадцатое	*vasyemnatsata-ye*
19th	девятнадцатое	*dyevyatnatsata-ye*
20th	двадцатое	*dvatsata-ye*
21st	двадцать первое	*dvatsat' pyerva-ye*
30th	тридцатое	*treetsata-ye*
31st	тридцать первое	*treetsat' pyerva-ye*

TIME

today	сегодня	*syevodnya*
yesterday	вчера	*fchyera*
tomorrow	завтра	*zaftra*
the day before yesterday	позавчера	*pazafchyera*
the day after tomorrow	послезавтра	*poslyezaftra*
this week	на этой неделе	*na etay nyedyel-ye*
last week	на прошлой неделе	*na proshlay nyedyel-ye*
next week	на следующей неделе	*na slyedoo-yoosheey nyedyel-ye*
this morning	сегодня утром	*syevodnya ootram*
this afternoon	сегодня днём	*syevodnya dnyom*
this evening/ tonight	сегодня вечером	*syevodnya vyechyeram*
yesterday afternoon	вчера днём	*fchyera dnyom*
last night *(before midnight)*	вчера вечером	*fchyera vyechyerom*
last night *(after midnight)*	вчера ночью	*fchyera noch'yoo*
tomorrow morning	завтра утром	*zaftra ootram*
tomorrow night	завтра вечером	*zaftra vyechyerom*
in three days	через три дня	*chyeryez tree dnya*
three days ago	три дня назад	*tree dnya nazat*
late	поздно	*pozna*
early	рано	*rana*
soon	скоро	*skora*
later on	позже	*pozhe*
at the moment	сейчас	*seeychas*
second	секунда	*seekoonda*
minute	минута	*meenoota*
one minute	одна минута	*adna meenoota*
two minutes	две минуты	*dvye meenooti*

quarter of an hour	четверть часа	*chyetvyert' chasa*
half an hour	полчаса	*polchasa*
three quarters of an hour	три четверти часа	*tree chyetvyertee chasa*
hour	час	*chas*
that day	тот день	*tot dyen,*
every day	каждый день	*kazhdi dyen'*
all day	весь день	*vyes' dyen'*
the next day	следующий день	*slyedoo-yooshshee dyen'*

TELLING THE TIME

One o'clock is час (*chas*); for two, three and four o'clock, use the number followed by часа (*chasa*). The remaining hours to twelve o'clock are simply the appropriate number plus the word часов (*chasov*).

For time past the hour, eg twenty past one, Russians say двадцать минут второго (*dvatsat' meenoot ftarova*) meaning literally 'twenty minutes of the second (hour)'.

Quarter past and half past one are also expressed as being 'of the following (hour)'. Quarter past one is therefore четверть второго (*chyetvyert' ftarova*) and half past two is половина третьего (*palaveena tryet'yeva*).

For time 'to' the hour, Russians use без (*byez*) meaning 'less', eg ten to three is без десяти три (*byez dyesyatee tree*), literally 'less ten three'.

The 24-hour clock is commonly used, in particular for timetables. Cross-reference to the number section on page 15 may prove helpful.

am	утра	*ootra*
pm	дня	*dnya*
one o'clock	час	*chas*
ten past one	десять минут второго	*dyesyat' meenoot ftarova*

quarter past one	четверть второго	*chyetvyert' ftarova*
half past one	половина второго	*palaveena ftarova*
twenty to two	без двадцати два	*byez dvatsatee dva*
quarter to two	без четверти два	*byez chyetvyertee dva*
two o'clock	два часа	*dva chasa*
13.00	тринадцать ноль-ноль	*treenatsat' nol'-nol'*
16.30	шестнадцать тридцать	*shesnatsat' treetsat'*
at half past five	в половине шестого	*fpalaveen-ye shestova*
at seven o'clock	в семь часов	*fsyem' cha'sof*
noon	полдень	*poldyen'*
midnight	полночь	*polnach'*

HOTELS

In recent years, the choice and standard of hotel accommodation in the big cities has improved significantly with the emergence of Western-managed hotels offering, in general, excellent standards of service. However, these are usually quite expensive, and a typical package tour is more likely to involve a stay in a traditional 'ex-Soviet' hotel (one that used to be state-run), particularly outside the big cities. This kind of package tour will usually include a generous, if not culinarily varied, breakfast, lunch and dinner, plus a room with en suite bathroom and telephone. Standards of service, courtesy and cleanliness vary but, compared to those of Western European hotels, are not likely to be more than adequate. Acting as a receptionist on each floor of the hotel, there will be a комсьержка (*kahs'yerzhka*) who will have custody of the keys and who will issue a key pass which will need to be shown when collecting the key. She will be able to help with any problem to do with your accommodation, laundry or simply make you a cup of tea.

Even if you are paying for your hotel accommodation with a credit card, you should always have a certain amount of foreign currency with you (preferably US dollars). You will need to exchange quite a lot of this foreign currency during your stay in Russia since shops, restaurants and bars will now only accept payment in roubles.

Throughout the day it is possible to have a light snack and tea or coffee in one of the hotel cafeterias. Travellers requiring a vegetarian menu should notify their tour guide or inform the hotel staff when checking in.

USEFUL WORDS AND PHRASES

balcony	балкон	*balkon*
bathroom	ванная	*vana-ya*
bed	кровать	*kravat'*

bedroom	спальня	*spal'nya*
bill	счёт	*shyot*
breakfast	завтрак	*zaftrak*
dining room	столовая	*stalova-ya*
dinner	ужин	*oozheen*
double room	номер с	*nomyer sdvoo-*
	двуспальной	*spal'nay*
	кроватью	*kravat'-yoo*
floor-lady	комсьержка	*kahs'yerzhka*
foyer	фойе	*fay-ye*
full board	проживание с	*prazheevaneeye*
	трёхразовым	*stryokh-razovim*
	питанием	*peetaneeyem*
half board	проживание с	*prazheevaneeye*
	двухразовым	*sdvookh-razovim*
	питанием	*peetaneeyem*
hotel	гостиница	*gasteeneetsa*
key	ключ	*klyooch*
lift	лифт	*leeft*
lunch	обед	*abyet*
manager	администратор	*admeeneestrator*
reception	ресепшен	*'reception'*
restaurant	ресторан	*ryestaran*
room	номер	*nomyer*
room service	комнатное	*komnatna-ye*
	обслуживание	*absloozheevaneeye*
shower	душ	*doosh*
single room	одноместный	*adnamyestni*
	номер	*nomyer*
toilet	туалет	*too-alyet*
twin room	двухместный	*dvookhmyestni*
	номер	*nomyer*

Do you have a larger/brighter room?
У вас есть номер побольше/посветлее?
oo vas yest' nomyer pabol'shye/pasvyetlyeye

Please could I have the key for room number …?
Дайте, пожалуйста, ключ от номера …
dayt-ye, pazhalsta, klooch ot nomyera

I'd prefer a room with a balcony
Я предпочёл (m)/предпочла (f) бы номер с балконом
ya pryedpachyol/pryedpachla bi nomyer sbalkonam

Is there satellite/cable TV in the rooms?
В номерах есть спутниковое/кабельное телевидение?
vnameerakh yesti spootheekavaye/kabeel'naye tyelyeveedeeneeye

The window in my room is jammed
Окно в моём номере не открывается
akno vmayom nomyer-ye nye atkriva-yetsa

The shower doesn't work
Душ не работает
doosh nye rabota-yet

The bathroom light doesn't work
В ванной нет света
v-vanay nyet svyeta

Can I have another light bulb?
Дайте другую лампочку
dayt-ye droogooyoo lampachkoo

There is no hot water/toilet paper
Нет горячей воды/туалетной бумаги
nyet garyachyay vadi/ too-alyetnay boomagee

What is the charge per night?
Сколько стоит номер за ночь?
skol'ka sto-eet nomyer zanach'

When is breakfast?
Когда завтрак?
kagda zaftrak

Would you have my luggage brought up?
Будьте добры, принесите мой багаж
bood't-ye dabri, preenyeseet-ye moy bagazh

Please call me at … o'clock
Пожалуйста, позвоните мне в … часов/часа
pazhalsta, pazvaneet-ye mnye v … chasof/chasa

Can I have breakfast in my room?
Можно завтракать в номере?
mozhna zavtrakat' vnomyer-ye

I'll be back at … o'clock
Я вернусь в …
ya vyernoos' v

My room number is …
Мой номер …
moy nomyer

I'm leaving tomorrow
Я уезжаю завтра
ya oo-yezha-yoo zaftra

At what time do I have to be out of my room?
Когда надо освободить номер?
kagda nada asvabadeet' nomyer

Can I have the bill, please?
Счёт, пожалуйста
shyot, pazhalsta

There has been some mistake, I asked for a double room
Произошла ошибка, я просил (m)/просила (f) номер с
  двуспальной кроватью
*pra-eezashla asheepka, ya praseel/praseela nomyer sdvoo-spal'nay
  kravat'yoo*

I'll pay by credit card
Я заплачу кредитной карточкой
ya zaplachoo kryedeetnay kartachkay

I'll pay cash
Я заплачу наличными
ya zaplachoo naleechnimee

Can you get me a taxi?
Вы можете вызвать мне такси?
vi mozhet-ye vizvat' mn-ye taksee

Thank you for all your help
Спасибо за вашу помощь
spaseeba za vashoo pomash'

THINGS YOU'LL HEAR

eezveeneet-ye, myest nyet
I'm sorry, we have no more places

adna-myestnikh namyerof bol'shye nyet
There are no single rooms left

dvookh-myestnikh namyerof bol'shye nyet
There are no twin rooms left

na skol'ka nachay?
For how many nights?

THINGS YOU'LL SEE

бар	*bar*	bar
ванная	*vana-ya*	bath
гостиница	*gasteeneetsa*	hotel
номер с двуспальной кроватью	*nomyer sdvoo-spal'nay kravat'-yoo*	double room
душ	*doosh*	shower
завтрак	*zaftrak*	breakfast
заказ	*zakas*	reservation
запасной выход	*zapasnoy vikhat*	emergency exit
к себе	*ksyeb-ye*	pull
лифт	*leeft*	lift
двухместный номер	*dvookh-myestni nomyer*	twin room
обед	*abyet*	lunch
одноместный номер	*adna-myestni nomyer*	single room
от себя	*atsyebya*	push
первый этаж	*pyervi etash*	ground floor
пожарный выход	*pazharni vikat*	fire exit
проживание с двухразовым питанием	*prazheevaneeye sdvookh-razavim peetanee-yem*	half board
проживание с трехразовым питанием	*prazheevaneeye stryokh-razavim peetaneeyem*	full board
регистратура	*ryegeestratoora*	reception
ресторан	*ryestaran*	restaurant
счёт	*shyot*	bill
туалет/W.C.	*too-alyet*	toilet
1		ground floor (*as shown on lift button*)

DRIVING

If you intend driving in Russia, you will need an international driving licence, international insurance documentation, and a car registration document.

Rough road conditions and relatively few garages make it essential to carry sufficient spares in case you have to do your own repairs. Some important items worth taking are a tow rope, engine oil, brake fluid, jump-start leads, spark plugs, spare windscreen wipers, spare bulbs, electric points and fuses, antifreeze in winter and a luminous warning triangle to place on the road in case you break down. Because it cannot be taken for granted that all garages sell the right petrol for your car, it is also worth taking a couple of petrol cans to stock up when you can and thus always have emergency supplies with you.

On the open road international (diagrammatic) road signs are used. The traffic police are called ГАИ (Ga-ee), which stands for State Automobile Inspectorate. If you are lost or in need of help they can, sometimes, be helpful. They can also fine you on the spot for violation of driving regulations.

Drive on the right and overtake on the left. On main roads out of town the speed limit is generally 90 km/h, and in town it is generally 60 km/h. Front passengers must wear their seat belts. It is a crime to drive a car after drinking any alcohol.

SOME COMMON ROAD SIGNS

автостанция	*avta-stantsee-ya*	garage
автостоянка	*avta-stayanka*	car park
автострада	*avta-strada*	motorway
бензоколонка	*byenzakalonka*	petrol station
берегись поезда	*byeryegees' poyezda*	beware of trains
включить фары	*vklyoocheet' fari*	headlights on
внимание!	*vneemaneeye!*	watch out!
вход воспрещён	*vkhod vaspryeshshyon*	no trespassing
выключить фары	*viklyoocheet' fari*	headlights off
въезд запрещён	*v-yezd zapryeshshyon*	no entry
гололёд	*galalyot*	sheet ice
держитесь	*dyerzheetyes'*	(pedestrians) keep
левой стороны	*lyevay starani*	to the left
дорожные работы	*darozhniye raboti*	roadworks
ж/д переезд	*zhe de pyerye-yezd*	level crossing
железно-	*zhelyezna-*	level crossing
дорожный	*darozhni*	
переезд	*pyerye-yezd*	
зона	*zona*	zone
конец автострады	*kanyets avta-stradi*	end of motorway
медленно	*myedlyenna*	slow
не обгонять	*nye abganyat'*	no overtaking
объезд	*ab-yezd*	diversion
одностороннее	*adna-staronyeye*	one-way street
движение	*dveezhyeneeye*	
опасно	*apasna*	danger
опасный	*apasni*	dangerous junction
перекрёсток	*pyeryekryostak*	
опасный поворот	*apasni pavarot*	dangerous bend
осторожно	*astarozhna*	caution
перекрёсток	*pyeryekryostak*	crossroads
пешеходы	*pyeshekhodi*	pedestrians
подземный	*padzyemni*	subway
переход	*pyeryekhot*	

→

скользко	skol'ska	slippery surface
скорая помощь	skora-ya pomashsh'	first aid
станция тех-обслуживания	stantsee-ya tyekh-absloozheevanee-ya	service station
стоянка запрещена	stayanka zapryeshshyena	no parking
центр города	tsyentr gorada	town centre
школа	shkola	school

USEFUL WORDS AND PHRASES

antifreeze	антифриз	anteefreez
automatic	автоматический	avta-mateechyeskee
boot	багажник	bagazhneek
brake (noun)	тормоз	tormas
breakdown	поломка	palomka
car	машина	masheena
caravan	дом-автофургон	dom-avtafoorgon
car seat (for a baby)	детское сиденье	dyetskaye seedyen
clutch	сцепление	stsyeplyeneeye
crossroads	перекрёсток	pyeryekryostak
to drive	водить машину	vadeet' masheenoo
engine	мотор	mator
exhaust	выхлопная труба	vikhlapna-ya trooba
fanbelt	вентиляционный ремень	vyenteelyatsee-oni ryemyen'
garage (for repairs)	автостанция	avta-stantsee-ya
garage (for petrol)	бензоколонка	byenzakalonka
gear	передача	pyeryedacha
junction (on motorway)	развилка	razveelka
licence	водительские права	vadeetyel'skeeye prava
(head) lights	фары	fari

(*rear*) lights	задние фонари	*zadneeye fanaree*
lorry	грузовик	*groozaveek*
motoring	автомобильный	*avtamabeel'ni*
manual	справочник	*spravachneek*
mirror	зеркало	*zyerkala*
motorbike	мотоцикл	*matatseekl*
motorway	автострада	*avta-strada*
number plate	номерной знак	*namyernoy znak*
petrol	бензин	*byenzeen*
road	дорога	*daroga*
to skid	заносить	*zanaseet'*
spares	запчасти	*zapchastee*
speed (*noun*)	скорость	*skorast'*
speed limit	ограничение	*agraneechyeneeye*
	скорости	*skorastee*
speedometer	спидометр	*speedomyetr*
steering wheel	руль	*rool'*
to tow	буксировать	*bookseeravat'*
traffic lights	светофор	*svyetafor*
trailer	прицеп	*preetsyep*
tyre	шина	*sheena*
van	фургон	*foorgon*
wheel	колесо	*kalyeso*
windscreen	лобовое стекло	*labavoye styeklo*

I'd like some oil/water
Мне нужно масло/нужна вода
mnye noozhna masla/noozhna vada

Fill it up, please!
Полный бак, пожалуйста!
polni bak, pazhalsta!

I'd like 10 litres of petrol
Мне нужно 10 литров бензина
mnye noozhna dyesyat' leetraf byenzeena

Would you check the tyres, please?
Проверьте шины, пожалуйста
pravyer't-ye sheeni, pazhalsta

Do you do repairs?
Здесь можно починить машину?
zdyes' mozhna pacheeneet' masheenoo

Can you repair the brakes?
Вы можете починить тормоза?
vi mozhet-ye pacheeneet' tarmaza

How long will it take?
Сколько времени это займёт?
skol'ka vryemyenee eta zImyot

Where can I park?
Где можно поставить машину?
gdye mozhna pastaveet' masheenoo

Can I park here?
Можно здесь поставить машину?
mozhna zdyes' pastaveet' masheenoo

There is something wrong with the engine
Что-то случилось с мотором
shto-ta sloocheelas' smatoram

The engine is overheating
Мотор перегревается
mator pyerye-gryeva-yetsa

I need a new tyre
Мне нужна новая шина
mnye noozhna nova-ya sheena

I'd like to hire a car
Я хочу взять напрокат машину
ya khach<u>oo</u> vzyat' naprak<u>a</u>t mash<u>ee</u>noo

Can we hire a baby/child seat? (car seat)
Здесь можно взять напрокат детское сиденье в машину?
Zdyes' mozhna vzyat' naprakat dyetskaye seedyen'ye vmasheenoo

Where is the nearest garage?
Где ближайшая автостанция?
gdye bleezh<u>I</u>sha-ya avta-st<u>a</u>ntsee-ya

How do I get to …?
Как доехать до …?
kak da-<u>ye</u>khat' do

Is this the road to …?
Это дорога в …?
<u>*eta dar<u>o</u>ga v*</u>

THINGS YOU'LL SEE

бензин	*byenz<u>ee</u>n*	petrol
бензоколонка	*byenzakal<u>o</u>nka*	petrol station
выход	*v<u>i</u>khot*	exit
ГАИ	*ga-ee*	traffic police
давление в шинах	*davl<u>ye</u>neeye vsh<u>ee</u>nakh*	tyre pressure
дизель	*d<u>ee</u>zyel'*	diesel
масло	*m<u>a</u>sla*	oil
развилка	*razv<u>ee</u>lka*	motorway junction
ремонт	*ryem<u>o</u>nt*	repair
автостанция	*avta-st<u>a</u>ntsee-ya*	garage (for repairs)

31

DIRECTIONS YOU MAY BE GIVEN

pryama	straight on
slyeva	on the left
pavyerneet-ye nalyeva	turn left
sprava	on the right
pavyerneet-ye naprava	turn right
pyervi pavarot naprava	first on the right
ftaroy pavarot nalyeva	second on the left
posl-ye …	past the …

THINGS YOU'LL HEAR

vi khateet-ye safta-mateecheskeem eelee roochnim oopravlyeneeyem?
Would you like an automatic or a manual?

pakazheet-ye vashi prava
May I see your licence?

RAIL TRAVEL

On long-distance journeys, tourists will usually travel in мягкий (*myakhkee*; literally 'soft') compartments with two sleeping berths or in купе (*koope*; literally 'coupé') compartments with four sleeping berths. In addition, there are are usually cheaper 'seat only' tickets available. All compartments are non-smoking unless passengers agree to the contrary. Travellers on the long-distance trains should be wary of thieves. Always lock your compartment door before you go to sleep.

The carriage attendant is there as a sort of maître d'hôtel cum chambermaid. He or she is responsible for (and house-proud of) the cleanliness of the carriage, and also makes up the beds, and serves tea. When not busy working (and frequently also when they are), they usually enjoy a good chat.

Tickets for long-distance journeys should always be booked in advance. It is probably best to arrange this through your travel agent. Buying tickets for suburban trains, on the other hand, can be done as easily as in the West.

USEFUL WORDS AND PHRASES

booking office	касса	*kasa*
buffet	буфет	*boofyet*
carriage	вагон	*vagon*
compartment	купе	*koope*
connection	пересадка	*pyeryesadka*
dining car	вагон-ресторан	*vagon-ryestaran*
emergency cord	стоп-кран	*stop-kran*
entrance	вход	*fkhot*
exit	выход	*vikhot*
to get in	входить	*fkhadeet'*
to get out	выходить	*vikhadeet'*
guard	проводник	*pravadneek*
indicator board	табло	*tablo*
left luggage (*office*)	камера хранения	*kamyera khranyenee-ya*

lost property office	бюро находок	byooro nakhodak
luggage rack	багажная полка	bagazhna-ya polka
luggage trolley	тележка для багажа	tyelyezhka dlya bagazha
luggage van	багажное отделение	bagazhna-ye atdyelyeneeye
platform	платформа	platforma
by rail	поездом	po-yezdam
railway	железная дорога	zhelyezna-ya daroga
reserved seat	забронированное место	zabraneeravano-ye myesta
restaurant car	вагон-ресторан	vagon-ryestaran
return ticket	обратный билет	abratni beelyet
seat	место	myesta
single ticket	билет в один конец	beelyet vadeen kanyets
sleeping car	спальный вагон	spal'ni vagon
station (main-line terminal)	вокзал	vagzal
station (all other stations including underground)	станция	stantsee-ya
station master	начальник вокзала	nachal'neek vagzala
ticket	билет	beelyet
ticket collector	контролёр	kantralyor
timetable	расписание	raspeesaneeye
tracks	пути	pootee
train	поезд	po-yest
waiting room	зал ожидания	zal azheedanee-ya
window	окно	akno

When does the train for … leave?
Когда отходит поезд в ...?
kagda atkhodeet po-yest v

When does the train from … arrive?
Когда приходит поезд из …?
agda preekhodeet po-yest eez

When is the next train to …?
Когда следующий поезд в …?
agda slyedoo-yoo-shshee po-yest v

When is the first train to …?
Когда первый поезд в …?
agda pyervi po-yest v

When is the last train to …?
Когда последний поезд в …?
agda paslyednee po-yest v

What is the fare to …?
Сколько стоит проезд до …?
skol'ka sto-eet pro-yest do

Do I have to change?
Мне нужно делать пересадку?
nnye noozhna dyelat' pyeryesadkoo

Does the train stop at …?
Поезд останавливается в …?
po-yest astanavleeva-yetsa v

How long does it take to get to …?
Сколько времени нужно ехать до …?
skolka vryemyenee noozhna yekhat' do

A return ticket to … please
Билет до … и обратно, пожалуйста
beelyet do …ee abratna pazhalsta

Do I have to pay a supplement?
Я должен (m)/должна (f) доплатить?
ya dolzhen/dalzhna daplateet'

Is there a reduction for children?
Есть ли скидка для детей?
yest' lee skeetna dlyadyetyey

Do we have to pay for the children?
Мы должны платить за детей?
mi dolzhni plateet' zadyeetyey

I'd like to reserve a seat
Я хочу заказать место
ya khachoo zakazat' myesta

Is this the right train for …?
Это поезд до …?
eta po-yest do

Is this the right platform for the … train?
С этой платформы отходит поезд до …?
setay platformi atkhodeet po-yest do

Which platform for the … train?
С какой платформы отходит поезд до …?
skakoy platformi atkhodeet po-yest do

Is the train late?
Поезд опаздывает?
po-yest apazdiva-yet

Could you help me with my luggage, please?
Вы не поможете мне с багажом, пожалуйста
vi nye pamozhet-ye mnye sbagazhom, pazhalsta

Is this seat free?
Это место свободно?
eta myesta svabodna

This seat is taken
Это место занято
eta myesta zanyata

I have reserved this seat
Я забронировал *(m)*/забронировала *(f)* это место
ya zabraneeravol/zabra neeravala eta myesta

May I open the window?
Можно открыть окно?
mozhna atkrit' akno

May I close the window?
Можно закрыть окно?
mozhna zakrit' akno

When do we arrive in …?
Когда мы приезжаем в ...?
kagda mi pree-yezha-yem v

What station is this?
Какая это станция?
kaka-ya eta stantsee-ya

What station (*main-line terminal*) is this?
Какой это вокзал?
kakoy eta vagzal

Do we stop at …?
Мы останавливаемся в ...?
mi astanavleeva-yemsa v

Is there a restaurant car on this train?
В этом поезде есть вагон-ресторан?
vetam po-yezd-ye yest' vagon-ryestaran

THINGS YOU'LL SEE

билетная касса	*beelyetna-ya kasa*	ticket office
билеты	*beelyeti*	tickets
буфет	*boofyet*	snack bar
вагон	*vagon*	carriage
вокзал	*vagzal*	central station (*main-line railway terminal*)
воскресные и праздничные дни	*vaskryesyesniye ee prazneechniye dnee*	Sundays and public holidays
вход	*fkhot*	entrance
выход	*vikhot*	exit
газеты	*gazyeti*	newspapers
доплата	*daplata*	supplement
задержка	*zadyershka*	delay
зал ожидания	*zal azheedanee-ya*	waiting room
занято	*zanya-ta*	engaged
информация	*eenformatsee-ya*	information
камера хранения	*kamyera khranyenee-ya*	left luggage
к поездам	*k po-yezdam*	to the trains
кроме воскресений	*krom-ye vaskryesyenee*	Sundays excepted
место для курения	*myesta dlya kooryenee-ya*	smoking permitted
не высовываться из окон	*nye visovivatsa eez okan*	do not lean out of the window
не курить	*nye kooreet'*	no smoking
не останав- ливается в ...	*nye astanav- leeva-yetsa v*	does not stop in ...

→

нет входа	*nyet fkhoda*	no entry
обмен валюты	*abmyen valyooti*	currency exchange
отправление	*atpravlyeneeye*	departures
платформа	*platforma*	platform
поездка	*pa-yestka*	journey
предварительный заказ билетов	*pryedvareetyel'ni zakas beelyetaf*	seat reservation
прибытие	*preebiteeye*	arrivals
пригородный поезд	*preegaradni po-yest*	local train
расписание	*raspeesaneeye*	timetable
свободно	*svabodna*	vacant
спальный вагон	*spal'ni vagon*	sleeping car
стоп-кран	*stop-kran*	emergency cord
только по будним дням	*tol'ka paboodneem dnyam*	weekdays only

THINGS YOU'LL HEAR

vneemaneeye
Attention

beelyeti, pazhalsta
Tickets, please

AIR TRAVEL

British Airways and Aeroflot both operate direct flights from London to Russia. Many national and local airlines make internal flights in Russia; the two biggest are Aeroflot and Transaero. Check that you have all necessary flight information, and in any case of doubt ask your travel agent to provide you with flight details in English and, if possible, in writing.

Before making arrangements to fly in Russia, you should first check that your visa permits you to travel to where you want to go. Be sure that you receive your ticket in good time and fully understand the flight details. You should make all necessary arrangements for accommodation prior to departure.

USEFUL WORDS AND PHRASES

aircraft	самолёт	*samalyot*
airline	авиакомпания	*aveea-kampaneeya*
airport	аэропорт	*aeraport*
arrival	прибытие	*preebiteeye*
baggage claim	выдача багажа	*vidacha bagazha*
boarding pass	посадочный талон	*pasadachni talon*
check-in (*noun*)	регистрация	*ryegeestratsee-ya*
check-in desk	стойка регистрации	*stoyka ryegeestratsee*
customs	таможня	*tamozhnya*
delay	задержка	*zadyershka*
departure	отправление	*atpravlyeneeye*
departure lounge	зал вылета	*zal vilyeta*
emergency exit	запасной выход	*zapasnoy vikhat*
fire exit	пожарный выход	*pazharni vikhat*
flight	рейс	*ryays*
flight number	номер рейса	*nomyer ryaysa*
gate	выход на посадку	*vikhad na pasadkoo*
jet	реактивный самолёт	*rye-akteevni samalyot*
land (*verb*)	приземлиться	*preezyemleet'sa*

long-distance flight	рейс дальнего следования	*ryays dal'nyeva slyeda-vanee-ya*
passport	паспорт	*paspart*
passport control	паспортный контроль	*paspartni kantrol'*
pilot	пилот	*peelot*
runway	взлётно-посадочная полоса	*vzlyotna-pasadachna-ya palasa*
seat	место	*myesta*
seat belt	ремень	*ryemyen'*
steward	бортпроводник	*bort-pravadneek*
stewardess	стюардесса	*styoo-ardesa*
take-off (*noun*)	взлёт	*vzlyot*
window	окно	*akno*
wing	крыло	*krilo*

When is there a flight to …?
Когда рейс в …?
kagda ryays v

What time does the flight to … leave?
Когда вылетает самолёт в …?
kagda vilyeta-yet samalyot v

Is it a direct flight?
Это прямой рейс?
eta pryamoy ryays

Do I have to change planes?
Я должен (*m*)/должна (*f*) пересесть на другой самолет?
ya dolzhen/dolzhna pyeryesyest' na droogoy samalyot

I'd like a single ticket to …
Дайте, пожалуйста, билет в один конец до …
dIt-ye, pazhalsta beelyet vadeen kanyets do

When do I have to check in?
Когда я должен (*m*)/должна (*f*) быть в аэропорту для
   регистрации?
kagda ya dolzhen/dolzhna bit' vaeraportoo dlya ryegeestratsee

I'd like a return ticket to …
Дайте, пожалуйста, билет в оба конца до ...
dIt-ye, pazhalsta beelyet voba kantsa do

I'd like a non-smoking seat, please
Я хочу место в отделении для некурящих
ya khachoo myesta vatdyelyenee dlya nyekooryashsheekh

I'd like a window seat, please
Я хочу место у окна, пожалуйста
ya khachoo myesta oo akna, pazhalsta

How long will the flight be delayed?
На сколько задерживается рейс?
na skol'ka zadyerzheeva-yetsa ryays

Which gate for the flight to …?
Какой выход на посадку на рейс до ...?
kakoy vikhad na pasadkoo na ryays do

When do we arrive in …?
Когда мы прилетаем в ...?
kagda mi preelyetayem v

May I smoke now?
Теперь можно курить?
tyepyer' mozhna kooreet'

I do not feel very well
Мне плохо
mnye plokha

THINGS YOU'LL SEE

Аэрофлот	*aeraflot*	Aeroflot
бортпроводник	*bort-pravadneek*	steward
выдача багажа	*vidacha bagazha*	baggage claim
вынужденная посадка	*vinoozhdyennaya pasadka*	emergency landing
высота	*visata*	altitude
выход на посадку	*vikhod na pasadkoo*	gate
задержка	*zadyershka*	delay
запасной выход	*zapasnoy vikhot*	emergency exit
информация	*eenformatsee-ya*	information
местное время	*myestna-ye vryemya*	local time
не курить	*nye kooreet'*	no smoking
отправление	*atpravlyeneeye*	departures
паспортный контроль	*paspartni kantrol'*	passport control
пассажиры	*pasazheeri*	passengers
пожарный выход	*pazharni vikhot*	fire exit
прибытие	*preebiteeye*	arrivals
пристегните ремни	*pree-styegneet-ye ryemnee*	fasten seat belts
прямой рейс	*pryamoy ryays*	direct flight
регистрация	*ryegeestratsee-ya*	check-in
регулярный рейс	*ryegoolyarni ryays*	scheduled flight
рейс	*ryays*	flight
самолёт	*samalyot*	aircraft
скорость	*skorast'*	speed
стюардесса	*styoo-ardesa*	stewardess
таможенный контроль	*tamozheni kantrol'*	customs control
транзитная посадка	*tranzeetna-ya pasadka*	intermediate stop
явиться на регистрацию	*yaveet'sa na ryegeestratsee-yoo*	to check in

THINGS YOU'LL HEAR

abyavlya-yetsa pasadka na ryays ...
The flight for ... is now boarding

pazhalsta, prIdeet-ye na pasadkoo k vikhadoo nomyer ...
Please go now to gate number ...

LOCAL PUBLIC TRANSPORT AND TAXIS

A single ride on a bus, tram or trolleybus costs a flat fare equivalent to no more than a few pence. It is cheapest to buy your tickets in a booklet of ten, called a книжечка (*kneezhechka*), which can be bought from the driver, or at a newspaper kiosk. Validate your ticket for the ride by perforating it in one of the punches hanging from the wall.

Bus stops have a yellow sign marked 'A' and trolleybus stops have a white sign marked 'T'. These transport services and the underground run from about 6 am to about midnight. For people staying in Moscow or St Petersburg for three or more weeks, it may be worth getting a monthly season ticket – единый (*yedeeni*) – which is valid on all forms of public transport, including the underground. The *yedeeni*, however, is only valid for a calendar month (so from mid-January to mid-February it probably would not be worth having because you would need to buy two).

Underground tokens – жетоны (*zhetoni*) – are bought from ticket offices in the station. However, tokens are currently being replaced by magnetic single- or multiple-trip tickets. The flat fare is relatively cheap compared to fares in Western Europe. To leave the underground, follow the выход в город (*vikhat vgorat*) signs, which mean 'Exit to the city'.

When you need to use the underground, it is probably worth writing down the name of your destination to help identify it in Cyrillic. To change lines, look for the sign переход на поезда до станций (*pyeryekhod na pa-yezda do stantsee …*), meaning 'Change to trains for stations …'.

Available taxis can be identified by a green light in the front of the windscreen. If you want to book a taxi it is wise to let your hotel do it for you as most operators don't speak English. Official taxis in Moscow and St Petersburg are yellow. Official taxis have meters, but they may be out-of-date and the driver might prefer to negotiate a price beforehand. Frequently, unofficial taxi drivers offer to pick you up, but it is not

recommended. Treat tipping just as you would do at home.
  Some of the expressions below would be suitable for
travellers going on a boat-trip.

USEFUL WORDS AND PHRASES

adult	взрослый	*vzrosli*
bus	автобус	*aftoboos*
bus stop	остановка автобуса	*astanofka aftoboosa*
child	ребёнок	*ryebyonak*
coach	автобус	*aftoboos*
conductor	кондуктор	*kandooktar*
connection	пересадка	*pyeryesatka*
cruise	круиз	*kroo-eez*
driver	водитель	*vadeetyel'*
fare	стоимость проезда	*sto-eemast' pra-yezda*
ferry	паром	*parom*
lake	озеро	*ozyera*
network map	схема	*skhyema*
number 5 bus	пятый автобус	*pyati aftoboos*
passenger	пассажир	*pasazheer*
quay	пристань	*preestan'*
river	река	*ryeka*
sea	море	*mor-ye*
seat	место	*myesta*
ship	теплоход	*tyeplakhot*
station	станция	*stantsee-ya*
subway	подземный переход	*padzyemni pyeryekhot*
taxi	такси	*taksee*
terminal	конечный пункт	*kanyechni poonkt*
ticket	билет	*beelyet*
tram	трамвай	*tramvi*
underground	метро	*myetro*

Where is the nearest underground station?
Где ближайшая станция метро?
gdye bleezhisha-ya stantsee-ya myetro

Where is the bus station?
Где автобусная станция?
gdye aftoboosna-ya stantsee-ya

Where is there a bus stop?
Где остановка автобуса?
gdye astanofka aftoboosa

Which buses go to …?
Какие автобусы идут до ...?
kakeeye aftoboosi eedoot do

How often do the buses go to …?
Как часто ходят автобусы в ...?
kak chasta khodyat aftoboosi v

Would you tell me when we get to …?
Скажите, пожалуйста, когда мы приедем в ...?
skazheet-ye, pazhalsta, kagda mi pree-yedyem v

Do I have to get off yet?
Мне пора выходить?
mnye para vikhadeet'

How do you get to …?
Как добраться до ...?
kak dabrat'sa do

Is it very far?
Это далеко?
eta dalyeko

I want to go to …
Я хочу поехать в …
ya khach_oo_ pa-y_e_khat' v

Do you go near …?
Вы едете в сторону …?
vi y_e_dyet-ye fst_o_ranoo

Where can I buy a ticket?
Где можно купить билет?
gdye mozhna koop_ee_t' beely_e_t

Could you close/open the window?
Закройте/откройте окно, пожалуйста?
zakr_oy_t-ye/atkr_oy_t-ye akn_o_, pazh_a_lsta

Could you help me get a ticket?
Вы не поможете мне купить билет?
vi nye pam_o_zhet-ye mnye koop_ee_t' beely_e_t

When does the last bus leave?
Когда отходит последний автобус?
kagd_a_ atkh_o_deet pasly_e_dnee aft_o_boos

THINGS YOU'LL HEAR

beely_e_ti, pazh_a_lsta
Tickets, please

astar_o_zhna, dvy_e_ree zakriv_a_-yootsa!
Be careful, the doors are closing!

sly_e_doo-yooshaa-ya st_a_ntsee-ya …
The next station is …

THINGS YOU'LL SEE

билет	*beeleyet*	ticket
взрослые	*vzrosliye*	adults
вход	*fkhot*	entrance
дети	*dyetee*	children
запасной выход	*zapasnoy vikhat*	emergency exit
конечный пункт	*kanyechni poonkt*	terminal
контролёр	*kantralyor*	ticket inspector
маршрут	*marshroot*	route
места	*myesta*	seats
мест нет	*myest nyet*	full
не курить	*nye kooreet'*	no smoking
нет входа	*nyet fkhoda*	no entry
остановка	*astanofka*	stop
отправление	*atpravlyeneeye*	departures
пожарный выход	*pazharni vikhat*	fire exit
разговаривать	*razgavareevat'*	do not speak to
с водителем	*svadeetyelyem*	the driver
запрещается	*zapryeshsha-yetsa*	
стоянка такси	*sta-yanka taksee*	taxi rank

DOING BUSINESS

In addition to the usual information, your business card should state how you can be contacted from Russia. It is a good idea to have your business card and any literature about your company in both English and Russian. Telephone services have improved dramatically in recent years, but since the postal service is still slow, written communication is probably best sent by courier, fax or email.

If your delegation does not have a Russian speaker, make sure in advance that the Russian side will supply qualified translators at all meetings.

It will be handy to have some gifts with you for appropriate occasions. Even more than in the West, the key figure to impress is the top man. He and his senior colleagues should be treated with particular attentiveness, wherever possible by representatives of corresponding rank from your own company.

Clearly, personal tact and business experience best dictate how to handle personal relationships with your Russian partners. Do not insult them by arguing over payment for any hospitality they are providing. Equally, do not take for granted how attractive they find contact with Westerners. Apart from a widespread partiality for Western consumer goods, mention of future business trips to the West is, where appropriate, likely to prove a strong incentive to them to continue business relations.

Useful Words and Phrases

accept	принимать	*preeneemat'*
accountant	бухгалтер	*boogaltyer*
accounts department	бухгалтерия	*boogaltyeree-ya*
to advertise	рекламировать	*ryeklameeravat'*
advertisement	реклама	*ryeklama*

airfreight	воздушная доставка	*vazdooshna-ya dastafka*
bid	заявка	*za-yafka*
board (*of directors*)	правление	*pravlyeneeye*
brochure	брошюра	*brashyoora*
business card	карточка (визитная)	*kartachka (veezytnaya)*
chairman	председатель	*pryedsyedatyel'*
cheap	дешёвый	*dyeshyovi*
client	клиент	*klee-yent*
company	компания	*kampanee-ya*
computer	компьютер	*kampyootyer*
consumer	потребитель	*patryebeetyel'*
contract	договор	*dagavor*
cost	стоимость	*sto-eemast'*
customer	покупатель	*pakoopatyel'*
director	директор	*deeryektar*
discount	скидка	*skeetka*
documents	документы	*dakoomyenti*
down payment	аванс	*avans*
email	е-мэйл	*ee-mayl*
email address	адрес электронной почты	*adryes elektronay pochti*
engineer	инженер	*eenzhenyer*
executive	исполнитель	*eespalneetyel'*
expensive	дорогой	*daragoy*
exports	экспорт	*eksport*
fax	факс	*faks*
to import	импортировать	*eemporteeravat'*
imports	импорт	*eemport*
instalment	очередной взнос	*achyeryednoy vznos*
invoice	накладная	*nakladna-ya*
to invoice	выставить счёт	*vistaveet' shshyot*
letter	письмо	*pees'mo*

letter of credit	аккредитив	*akryedeeteev*
loss	потери	*patyeree*
manager	управляющий	*oopravlya-yooshee*
manufacture	изготовление	*eezgatavlyeneeye*
margin	маржа	*mar-zha*
market	рынок	*rinak*
marketing	маркетинг	*markyeteenk*
meeting	встреча	*fstryecha*
negotiations	переговоры	*pyeryegavori*
offer	предложение	*pryedlazheneeye*
order	заказ	*zakas*
to order	заказывать	*zakazivat'*
personnel	персонал	*pyersanal*
price	цена	*tsena*
product	продукция	*pradooktsee-ya*
production	производство	*pra-eezvotstva*
profit	прибыль	*preebil'*
promotion	продвижение	*pradveezheneeye*
(*publicity*)	с помощью	*spomashsh'yoo*
	рекламы	*ryeklami*
purchase order	закупочный заказ	*zakoopachni zakas*
sales department	отдел продаж	*atdyel pradazh*
sales director	директор по	*deeryektar po*
	продажам	*pradazham*
sales figures	статистика	*stateesteeka*
	продаж	*pradazh*
secretary	секретарь	*syekryetar'*
shipment	доставка морем	*dastafka moryem*
tax	налог	*nalok*
tender (*noun*)	тендер	*tender*
total	итог	*eetok*

My name is …
Меня зовут …
myenya zavoot

Here's my card
Вот моя карточка
vot ma-ya kartachka

Pleased to meet you
Рад (*m*)/рада (*f*) познакомиться
rad/rada paznakomeet'sa

May I introduce …?
Позвольте представить …
pazvol't-ye pryedstaveet'

My company is …
Моя компания …
maa-ya kampanee-ya

Our product is selling very well in the UK market
Наша продукция очень хорошо продаётся на
   британском рынке
*nasha pradooktsee-ya ochhyen' kharasho prada-yotsa na
   breetanskam rink-ye*

We are looking for partners in Russia
Мы ищем партнёров в России
mi eeshshem partnyoraf vrasee

At our last meeting …
На нашей последней встрече …
na nashay paslyednay fstryeche

10/25/50 per cent
десять/двадцать пять/пятьдесят процентов
dyesyat'/dvatsat' pyat'/pyadyeesyat pratsentaf

More than …
Больше чем …
bol'she chyem

Less than …
Меньше чем …
myen'she chyem

We're on schedule
Мы сделаем в срок
mi zdelayem vsrok

We're slightly behind schedule
Мы немного отстаём от сроков
mi nyeemnoga atsta-yom atsrokaf

Please accept our apologies
Пожалуйста, примите наши извинения
pazhalsta, preemeet-ye nashee eezveenyenee-ya

There are good government grants available
Имеются хорошие правительственные дотации
eemye-yootsa kharosheeye praveetyel'stvenniye datatsee

It's a deal
Договорились
dagavareelees'

I'll have to check that with my manager
Я должен (m)/я должна (f) обсудить это с менеджером
ya dolzhen/dalzhna absoodeet'eta smenedzheram

I'll get back to you on that
Мы вернемся к этому вопросу позже
mi vyernyomsya ketamu vaprosu pozhe

Our quote will be with you very shortly
Наши расценки вы получите в ближайшее время
*n*a*shee rastsenkee vi pal*oo*cheet-ye vbleezh*i*shye-ye vr*ye*mya*

We'll send them airfreight
Мы отправим ихсамолетом
*mi atpr*a*vim eech samoly*o*tom*

It's a pleasure to do business with you
Приятно иметь дело с вами
*pree-*ya*tna eem*ye*t' d*ye*la sv*a*mee*

**We look forward to a mutually beneficial business
  relationship**
Мы надеемся на взаимовыгодное деловое сотрудничество
*mi nadyeemsya na vza-eemav*i*gadnaye dyelav*o*ye saatr*oo*dneechyestva*

EATING OUT

The highest standards of service and food are found in the Western-managed hotels and restaurants in the big cities. However, prices tend to be quite high and the dishes generally more orientated to Western cuisine rather than Russian.

There are now a large number of private restaurants and cafés which in general offer good, and in some cases excellent, standards of both cuisine and service. Prices vary and you must now pay in roubles in all restaurants. Expect some form of live entertainment here in the evenings, ranging from classical music to topless cabaret. The best way to keep up-to-date with the restaurant scene is to read one of the free English-language newspapers (for instance, the *Moscow Tribune* or *Moscow Times*), normally available in hotel foyers.

Finally there are the state-run restaurants, where on the whole standards of service and cuisine have declined in recent years. Their principal attraction now is that most of them are still reasonably priced, meaning it is possible to eat a hearty meal with caviar and champagne without breaking the bank. However, these restaurants remain difficult to book, unless the restaurant in question happens to be in your hotel (as a resident you should assume that you are entitled to dine there).

To avoid disappointment it is always advisable to book your table at least one day in advance, even at the Western-managed restaurants. If you decide to book a table at a state-run restaurant you should start to make arrangements for this well in advance. It is also worthwhile trying to get in at the weekend since this is when the latter are at their liveliest.

St Petersburg justifiably prides itself on better culinary standards than Moscow, making the choice for the consumer wider. As in the West, restaurants' reputations fluctuate and it is always worth asking locals for the most up-to-date recommendations on eating out.

Apart from caviar, vodka (which is ordered by the gram in restaurants) and dry champagne, strongly recommended are the пельмени (*pyelmyenee*), блины (*bleeni*), щи (*shshi*), борщ (*borshsh*) and fresh fish. The best Soviet wines come from Georgia and the Crimea and the finest cognac is Armenian.

It is possible to eat very cheaply in more humble establishments, although the food might seem rather basic when compared to the West. The usual rule (as with Russian shops) is simply 'what you see is what you get'. The café – кафе (*kafe*) – is slightly more down-market than the restaurant, and the столовая (*stalova-ya*) is similar to a canteen.

Instant snacks are available at a закусочная (*zakoosachna-ya*). A пельменная (*pyel'myenna-ya*) serves meat dumplings and a шашлычная (*shashlichna-ya*) serves spicy meat on a skewer.

The пивной бар (*peevnoy bar*, literally 'beer bar') – the Russian version of a pub – serves a considerable range of beers, soft and alcoholic drinks and traditional Russian food (depending on the class). Traditional English and Irish pubs are now found as well (the most well-known and popular are John Bull and Rosie O'Grady's). The bars in the larger hotels offer a fair range of alcohol and cigarettes for consumption in surroundings that are usually fairly congenial.

USEFUL WORDS AND PHRASES

beer	пиво	*peeva*
bill	счёт	*shyot*
bottle	бутылка	*bootilka*
bowl	пиала	*peeala*
cake	пирог	*peerok*
caviar	икра	*eekra*
champagne	шампанское	*shampanska-ye*
chef	повар	*povar*
coffee	кофе	*kof-ye*
cup	чашка	*chashka*
fork	вилка	*veelka*
glass	стакан	*stakan*
knife	нож	*nosh*

menu	меню	*myenyoo*
milk	молоко	*malako*
mineral water	минеральная вода	*meenyeral'na-ya vada*
napkin	салфетка	*salfyetka*
plate	тарелка	*taryelka*
receipt	чек	*chyek*
sandwich	бутерброд	*bootyerbrot*
soup	суп	*soop*
spoon	ложка	*loshka*
sugar	сахар	*sakhar*
table	стол	*stol*
tea	чай	*chI*
teaspoon	чайная ложка	*chIna-ya loshka*
tip	чаевые	*cha-yeviye*
waiter	официант	*afeetsee-ant*
waitress	официантка	*afeetsee-antka*
water	вода	*vada*
wine	вино	*veeno*

A table for two, please
Стол на двоих, пожалуйста
stol na dva-eekh, pazhalsta

But I have ordered a table
Но я заказал (m)/заказала (f) стол
no ya zakazal/zakazala stol

But those tables are free
Но эти столы свободны
no etee stali svabodni

Can I see the menu?
Можно посмотреть меню?
mozhna pasmatryet' myenyoo

I would like to book a table for tomorrow evening
Я хочу заказать стол на завтрашний вечер
ya khach<u>oo</u> zakaz<u>a</u>t' stol na z<u>a</u>ftrashnee v<u>ye</u>chyer

What would you recommend?
Что вы посоветуете?
shto vi pasav<u>ye</u>too-yet-ye

Do you do children's portions?
Вы делаете детские порции?
vi dy<u>e</u>layetye dy<u>e</u>tskeeye p<u>o</u>rtsee-ee

Can you warm this bottle/baby food for me?
Вы не могли бы подогреть эту бутылку/корм для малыша?
vi nee maglee-bi padagryet etoo bootilkoo/korm olya malisha

Is there a highchair/baby changing room?
Здесь есть высокий стул/комната матери и ребенка?
zdyes yesti vis<u>o</u>keey stool/k<u>o</u>mnata m<u>a</u>tyeree eeryebyonka

Do you have a vegetarian menu?
У вас есть меню для вегетарианцев?
oov<u>a</u>s yest' myeny<u>oo</u> dlya vyegyetaree<u>a</u>ntsev

I'd like …
Я хочу ...
ya khach<u>oo</u>

100/200 grams of vodka, please
сто/двести граммов водки, пожалуйста
sto/dvy<u>e</u>stee gr<u>a</u>maf v<u>o</u>tkee, pazh<u>a</u>lsta

Just a cup of coffee, please
Просто чашку кофе, пожалуйста
pr<u>o</u>sta ch<u>a</u>shkoo k<u>o</u>f-ye, pazh<u>a</u>lsta

Waiter!
Официант!
afeetsee-ant

Can we have the bill, please?
Счёт, пожалуйста
shyot, pazhalsta

I only want a snack
Я хочу только закуску
ya khachoo tol'ka zakooskoo

I didn't order this
Я не заказывал (*m*)/заказывала (*f*) это
ya nye zakazival/zakazivala eta

May we have some more ...?
Можно ещё ...?
mozhna yeshyo

The meal was very good, thank you
Спасибо, было очень вкусно
spaseeba, bila ochyen' fkoosna

THINGS YOU'LL HEAR

pree-yatnava apyeteeta
Enjoy your meal

MENU GUIDE

STARTERS

блины с икрой (*bleeni seekroy*) — pancakes with caviar
блины со сметаной (*bleeni sa smyetanay*) — pancakes with sour cream
грибы в сметане (*greebi fsmyetan-ye*) — mushrooms in sour cream
грибы маринованые (*greebi mareenovaniye*) — marinated mushrooms
закуски (*zakooskee*) — starters
заливная рыба (*zaleevna-ya riba*) — fish in aspic
икра (*eekra*) — caviar
икра баклажанная (*eekra baklazhana-ya*) — aubergines with onions and tomatoes
икра зернистая (*eekra zyerneesta-ya*) — fresh caviar
икра кетовая (*eekra kyetova-ya*) — red caviar
кильки (*keel'kee*) — sprats
лососина (*lasaseena*) — salmon
осетрина заливная (*asyetreena zaleevna-ya*) — sturgeon in aspic
осетрина с гарниром (*asyetreena zgarneeram*) — sturgeon with garnish
сардины в масле (*sardeeni vmasl-ye*) — sardines in oil
сёмга (*syomga*) — salmon
солёные огурцы (*salyoniye agoortsi*) — pickled cucumbers
солёные помидоры (*salyoniye pameedori*) — pickled tomatoes
фаршированные помидоры (*farsheerovaniye pameedori*) — stuffed tomatoes

SOUPS

борщ (*borshsh*) — beef or pork, beetroot and cabbage soup
бульон с пирожками (*bool'yon speerashkamee*) — clear soup with small meat pies
бульон с фрикадельками (*bool'yon sfreekadyel'kamee*) — clear soup with meatballs
мясной бульон (*myasnoy bool'yon*) — clear meat soup
овощной суп (*avashnoy soop*) — vegetable soup
окрошка (*akroshka*) — cold summer soup
рассольник (*rasol'neek*) — pickled cucumber soup

солянка (*salyanka*) — spicy soup made from fish or meat and vegetables

суп из свежих грибов
(*soop eez svyezheekh greebof*) — fresh mushroom soup

суп картофельный (*soop kartofyel'ni*) — potato soup

суп-лапша с курицей (*soop lapsha skooreetsay*) — chicken noodle soup

суп мясной (*soop myasnoy*) — meat soup

суп томатный (*soop tamatni*) — tomato soup

уха (*ookha*) — fish soup

харчо (*kharcho*) — thick, spicy mutton soup from Georgia

щи (*shshee*) — cabbage soup

EGG DISHES

омлет натуральный (*amlyet natooral'ni*) — plain omelette

омлет с ветчиной (*amlyet svyetcheenoy*) — ham omelette

яичница-глазунья (*ya-eechneetsa glazoon'ya*) — fried eggs

яйца вкрутую (*yltsa fkrootoo-yoo*) — hard-boiled eggs

яйца всмятку (*yltsa fsmyatkoo*) — soft-boiled eggs

яйцо (*yltso*) — egg

яйцо под майонезом (*yltso pod mlanyezam*) — egg mayonnaise

FISH

ассорти рыбное (*asartee ribna-ye*) — assorted fish

жареная рыба (*zharyena-ya riba*) — fried fish

камбала (*kambala*) — plaice

карп с грибами (*karp zgreebamee*) — carp with mushrooms

кета (*kyeta*) — Siberian salmon

копчёная сёмга (*kapchyona-ya syomga*) — smoked salmon

осетрина под белым соусом
(*asyetreena pod byelim so-oosam*) — sturgeon in white sauce

осетрина с гарниром (*asyetreena zgarneeram*) — sturgeon with garnish

осетрина с пикантным соусом
(*asyetreena speekantnim so-oosam*) — sturgeon in piquant sauce

осётр, запечённый в сметане
(*asyotr zapyechyoni fsmyetan-ye*) — sturgeon baked in sour cream

палтус (*paltoos*) — halibut

печень трески в масле
(*pyechyen' tryeskee vmasl-ye*) — cod liver in oil

рыбные блюда (*ribniye blyooda*)   fish dishes
сельдь (*sye'ld'*)   herring
селёдка малосольная   slightly salted herring
    (*syelyodka malasol'na-ya*)
скумбрия запечённая   baked mackerel
    (*skoombree-ya zapyechyona-ya*)
судак в белом вине (*soodak vbyelam veen-ye*)   pike-perch in white wine
судак, жаренный в тесте   pike-perch fried in batter
    (*soodak zharyeni ftyest-ye*)
судак по-русски (*soodak pa-rooskee*)   pike-perch Russian style
треска (*tryeska*)   cod
тунец (*toonyets*)   tuna fish
фаршированная рыба (*farsheerovana-ya riba*)   stuffed fish
форель (*faryel'*)   trout
шпроты (*shproti*)   sprats
щука (*shshooka*)   pike

Meat Dishes

азу (*azoo*)   small pieces of meat in a savoury sauce

ассорти мясное (*asartee myasno-ye*)   assorted meats
тефтели (*tyeftyelee*)   meatballs
голубцы (*galooptsee*)   cabbage leaves stuffed with meat and rice

дичь (*deech*)   game
колбаса (*kalbasa*)   salami sausage, or boiled sausage
копчёная колбаса (*kapchyona-ya kalbasa*)   smoked sausage
мясо (*myasa*)   meat
печёнка (*pyechyonka*)   liver
почки (*pochkee*)   kidneys
рубленое мясо (*rooblyena-ye myasa*)   mince meat
рубленые котлеты (*rooblyeniye katlyeti*)   rissoles
сосиски (*saseeskee*)   frankfurters
студень (*stoodyen'*)   aspic
тефтели с рисом (*tyeftyelee sreesam*)   small meatballs with rice
филе (*feelye*)   fillet
шашлык (*shashlik*)   kebab

MENU GUIDE

Beef

антрекот (antryekot) — entrecôte steak

беф-строганов (byef-stroganaf) — beef Stroganoff

бифштекс натуральный (beefshtyeks natooral'ni) — fried or grilled beefsteak

говядина отварная с хреном (gavyadeena atvarna-ya skhryenam) — boiled beef with horseradish

говядина тушёная (gavyadeena tooshyona-ya) — stewed beef

гуляш из говядины (goolyash eez gavyadeeni) — beef goulash

котлеты с грибами (katlyeti zgreebamee) — steak with mushrooms

рагу из говядины (ragoo eez gavyadeeni) — beef ragout

ромштекс с луком (romshtyeks slookam) — steak with onion

ростбиф с гарниром (rostbeef zgarneeram) — cold roast beef with garnish

Lamb

баранина (barneena) — mutton, lamb

бараньи отбивные (baran'ee atbeevniye) — lamb chops

баранина на вертеле (barneena na vyertyel-ye) — mutton grilled on a skewer

битки из баранины (beetkee eez barninee) — lamb meat steaks

рагу из баранины (ragoo eez barneeni) — lamb ragout

шашлык из баранины (shashlik eez barneeni) — lamb kebab

Pork

буженина с гарниром (boozheneena sgarneeram) — cold boiled pork with garnish

ветчина (vyetching) — ham

картофель с ветчиной и шпиком (kartofyel' svyetchinoy ee shpeekam) — potatoes with ham and bacon fat

копчёные свиные рёбрышки с фасолью (kapchoniye sveeniye ryobrishkee sfasol'yoo) — smoked pork ribs with beans

окорок (okarak) — gammon

свинина жареная с гарниром (sveeneena zharyena-ya sgarneeram) — fried pork with garnish

свинина с квашеной капустой (sveeneena skvashenay kapoostay) — pork with sauerkraut

свиные отбивные с чесноком (sveeniye atbeevniye schesnakom) — pork chops with garlic

шашлык из свинины с рисом (shashlik eez sveeneeni sreesam) — pork kebab with rice

VEAL

битки (*beetkee*)	steaks or minced steaks
рулет из рубленой телятины (*roolyet eez rooblyenay tyelyateeni*)	minced veal roll
телятина (*tyelyateena*)	veal
телячьи отбивные (*tyelyach'ee atbeevni-ye*)	veal chops
фрикадели из телятины в соусе (*freekadyelee eez tyelyateeni vso-oos-ye*)	veal meatballs in gravy
шницель с яичницей-глазуньей (*shneetsyel' sya-eechneetsay glazoon'yay*)	schnitzel with fried egg

POULTRY

блюда из птицы (*blyooda eez pteetsi*)	poultry dishes
гусь жареный с капустой или яблоками (*goos' zharyeni skapoostay eelee yablakamee*)	roast goose with cabbage or apples
индейка (*indyayka*)	turkey
котлеты по-киевски (*katlyeti pa-kee-yefskee*)	chicken Kiev
пожарские котлеты (*pazharskiye katlyeti*)	minced chicken
курица (*kooreetsa*)	chicken
отварной цыплёнок (*atvarnoy tsiplyonak*)	boiled chicken
панированный цыпленок (*paneerovani tsiplyonak*)	chicken in breadcrumbs
птица (*pteetsa*)	poultry
утка (*ootka*)	duck
цыплёнок в тесте (*tsiplyonak ftyest-ye*)	chicken in a pastry
цыплёнок по-охотничьи (*tsiplyonak pa-akhotneech'ee*)	chicken chasseur
цыплёнок «табака» (*tsiplyonak tabaka*)	Caucasian chicken with garlic sauce
цыплёнок фрикасе (*tsiplyonak freekase*)	chicken fricassee
чахохбили (*chakhokhbeelee*)	chicken casserole Georgian style

PIES AND PASTRY DISHES

изделия из теста (*eezdyelee-ya eez tyesta*)	pastry dishes
пельмени (*pyel'myenee*)	meat dumplings
пирожок (*peerazhok*)	pie
пирожки (*peerashkee*)	pies
пирожки с капустой (*peerashkee skapoostay*)	pies filled with cabbage
пирожки с мясом (*peerashkee smyasam*)	pies filled with meat
пирожки с творогом (*peerashkee stvoragam*)	pies filled with cottage cheese
тесто (*tyesta*)	pastry

VEGETABLES

баклажан (*baklazhan*)	aubergine
жареный картофель (*zharyeni kartofyel'*)	fried potatoes
зелёный горошек (*zyelyoni garoshek*)	green peas
кабачки (*kabachkee*)	courgettes
капуста (*kapoosta*)	cabbage
картофель (*kartofyel'*)	potatoes
кислая капуста (*keesla-ya kapoosta*)	sauerkraut
лук (*look*)	onions, spring onions
морковь (*markof'*)	carrots
овощи (*ovashshchee*)	vegetables
огурец (*agooryets*)	cucumber
перец (*pyeryets*)	pepper
петрушка (*pyetrooshka*)	parsley
помидоры (*pameedori*)	tomatoes
с гарниром (*zgarneegram*)	with garnish
свёкла (*svyokla*)	beetroot
фасоль (*fasol'*)	French, haricot or kidney beans
цветная капуста (*tsvyetna-ya kapoosta*)	cauliflower
чеснок (*chyesnok*)	garlic

SALADS

винегрет (*veenyegryet*)	vegetable salad
зелёный салат (*zyelyoni salat*)	green salad
огурцы со сметаной (*agoortsi sa smyetanay*)	cucumber in sour cream
салат «Оливье» (*salat 'aleev'ye*)	'Oleev'ye' salad, mixed vegetable and meat salad
салат из лука (*salat eez looka*)	spring onion salad

салат из огурцов (*salat eez agoortsof*)   cucumber salad
салат из помидоров (*salat eez pameedoraf*)   tomato salad
салат из помидоров с брынзой   tomato salad with feta
  (*salat eez pameedoraf zbrinzay*)   cheese
салат из редиски (*salat eez ryedeeskee*)   radish salad
салат мясной (*salat myasnoy*)   meat salad
салат с крабами (*salat skrabamee*)   crab salad

PASTA AND RICE

вермишель (*vyermeeshel'*)   vermicelli
лапша (*lapsha*)   noodles
макароны (*makaroni*)   macaroni
плов (*plof*)   pilaf
рис (*rees*)   rice

BREAD

баранки (*barankee*)   ring-shaped rolls
белый хлеб (*byeli khlyep*)   white bread
бородинский хлеб (*baradeenskee khlyep*)   black rye bread
булки (*boolkee*)   rolls
бутерброд с сыром (*bootyerbrot s-siram*)   cheese sandwich
ржаной хлеб (*rzhanoy khlyep*)   black rye bread
хлеб (*khlyep*)   bread
чёрный хлеб (*chyorni khlyep*)   brown bread

CAKES AND DESSERTS

блинчики с вареньем   pancakes with jam
  (*bleencheekee svaryen'yem*)
блины (*bleeni*)   pancakes
блины со сметаной (*bleeni sa smyetanay*)   pancakes with sour cream
вареники (*varyeneekee*)   curd or fruit dumplings
ватрушка (*vatrooshka*)   curd tart
галушки (*galooshki*)   dumplings
десерт (*dyesyert*)   dessert
желе (*zhelye*)   jelly
кекс (*kyeks*)   fruit cake
кисель (*kisyel'*)   thin fruit jelly
кисель из клубники (*keesyel' eez kloobneekee*)   strawberry jelly

кисель из чёрной смородины (keesyel' eez chyornoy smarodeeni)	blackcurrant jelly
компот из груш (kampot eez groosh)	stewed pears
компот из сухофруктов (kampot eez sookha-frooktaf)	stewed dried fruit mixture
конфета (kanfyeta)	sweet
коржик (korzheek)	flat dry shortbread
крем (kryem)	butter cake filling
молочный кисель (malochni keesyel')	milk jelly
мороженое клубничное (marozhena-ye kloobneechna-ye)	strawberry ice cream
мороженое молочное (marozhena-ye malochna-ye)	dairy ice cream
мороженое молочное с ванилином (marozhena-yemalochna-ye svaneeleenam)	dairy ice cream with vanilla
мороженое «пломбир» (marozhena-ye plambeer)	ice cream "Plombir"
мороженое шоколадное (marozhena-ye shakaladna-ye)	chocolate ice cream
печенье (pyechyen'ye)	biscuits
пирожок с повидлом (peerazhok spadleevam)	pie with jam
пирог с яблоками (peerok syablakamee)	apple pie
пирожное (peerozhna-ye)	small cake
повидло (paveedla)	thick jelly
пончики (poncheekee)	doughnuts
салат из яблок (salat eez yablak)	apple salad
сдобное тесто (zdobna-ye tyesta)	sweet pastry
сладкое (sladka-ye)	dessert, sweet course
сырники (sirneekee)	cheesecakes
торт (tort)	cake, gateau
фруктовое мороженое (frooktova-yemarozhena-ye)	fruit ice cream
шоколад (shakalat)	chocolate
эскимо (eskeemo)	choc-ice

CHEESE

брынза (brinza)	feta cheese
плавленый сыр (plavlyeni sir)	processed cheese
сыр (sir)	cheese
творог (tvorog)	cottage cheese

FRUIT AND NUTS

абрикосы (*abreek<u>o</u>si*)	apricots
апельсины (*apyel's<u>ee</u>ni*)	oranges
арбуз (*arb<u>oos</u>*)	watermelon
банан (*ban<u>a</u>n*)	banana
виноград (*veenagr<u>a</u>t*)	grapes
грецкий орех (*gr<u>ye</u>tskee ar<u>ye</u>kh*)	walnut
груши (*gr<u>oo</u>shee*)	pears
дыня (*d<u>i</u>nya*)	melon
клубника (*kloobn<u>ee</u>ka*)	strawberries
лимон (*leem<u>o</u>n*)	lemon
малина (*mal<u>ee</u>na*)	raspberries
мандарины (*mandar<u>ee</u>ni*)	mandarins
орехи (*ar<u>ye</u>khee*)	nuts
персик (*p<u>ye</u>rseek*)	peach
сливы (*sl<u>ee</u>vi*)	plums
фрукты (*fr<u>oo</u>kti*)	fruit
черешня (*cher<u>ye</u>shnya*)	cherries
чёрная смородина (*ch<u>yo</u>rna-ya smar<u>o</u>deena*)	blackcurrant
яблоки (*y<u>a</u>blakee*)	apples

DRINKS

апельсиновый сок (*apyel's<u>ee</u>navi sok*)	orange juice
белое вино (*b<u>ye</u>la-ye veen<u>o</u>*)	white wine
вода (*vad<u>a</u>*)	water
водка (*v<u>o</u>dka*)	vodka
газированная вода (*gazeer<u>o</u>vana-ya vad<u>a</u>*)	soda water
игристое вино (*eegr<u>ee</u>sto-ye veen<u>o</u>*)	sparkling wine
квас (*kvas*)	kvas (non-alcoholic fizzy drink made of fermented bread and water)
кефир (*kyef<u>ee</u>yr*)	kefir (sour yoghurt drink)
коньяк (*kon'y<u>a</u>k*)	brandy
кофе с молоком (*k<u>o</u>f-ye smalak<u>o</u>m*)	coffee with milk
красное вино (*kr<u>a</u>sna-ye veen<u>o</u>*)	red wine
минеральная вода (*meenyer<u>a</u>l'na-ya vad<u>a</u>*)	mineral water
молоко (*malak<u>o</u>*)	milk
напитки (*nap<u>ee</u>tkee*)	drinks
перцовка (*pyerts<u>o</u>vka*)	pepper vodka
пиво (*p<u>ee</u>va*)	beer

десертное вино (*dyesyertnoye veeno*)   dessert wine
томатный сок (*tamatni sok*)   tomato juice
чай (*chI*)   tea
чай с лимоном (*chI sleemonam*)   lemon tea
чёрный кофе (*chyorni kof-ye*)   black coffee
шампанское (*shampanska-ye*)   champagne
яблочный сок (*yablachni sok*)   apple juice

BASIC FOODS

варенье (*varyen'ye*)   jam, preserves
горчица (*garcheetsa*)   mustard
гренки (*gryenkee*)   croutons
гречка (*gryechka*)   buckwheat
джем (*dzhem*)   jam
каша (*kasha*)   porridge
маргарин (*margareen*)   margarine
масло (*masla*)   butter, oil
мёд (*myot*)   honey
рассол (*rasol*)   pickle
сливки (*sleefkee*)   cream
сливочное масло (*sleevachna-ye masla*)   butter
сметана (*smyetana*)   sour cream
солёное печенье (*salyona-ye pyechyen'ye*)   savoury biscuit
соль (*sol'*)   salt
соус майонез (*so-oos mIanyes*)   mayonnaise sauce
соус хрен (*so-oos khryen*)   horseradish sauce
чёрный перец (*chorni pyeryets*)   black pepper
уксус (*ooksoos*)   vinegar

CULINARY METHODS OF PREPARATION

домашний (*damashnee*)   home-made
жареный (*zharyeni*)   grilled, fried or roast
жаренный на вертеле   grilled on a skewer
  (*zharyeni na vyertyel-ye*)
отварной (*atvarnoy*)   boiled, poached
печёный (*pyechyoni*)   baked
сырой (*siroy*)   raw
тушёный (*tooshyoni*)   stewed
фаршированный (*farsheerovani*)   stuffed

Menu Terms

блюдо (*bly<u>oo</u>da*) — dish, course

меню (*myen<u>yoo</u>*) — menu

национальные русские блюда — Russian traditional dishes
(*natseean<u>a</u>l'niye r<u>oo</u>skeeye bly<u>oo</u>da*)

горячее (*gar<u>ya</u>chyeye*) — main course

первое блюдо (*p<u>ye</u>rva-ye bly<u>oo</u>do*) — first course

русская кухня (*r<u>oo</u>ska-ya k<u>oo</u>khnya*) — Russian cuisine

фирменные блюда (*f<u>ee</u>rmyeniye bl<u>oo</u>da*) — speciality dishes

SHOPPING

If you are looking for presents to take home, then one option is to visit a Берёзка (*beryozka*) shop, selling mostly souvenirs, alcohol and tobacco. The most attractive goods are blue and white Gzhel crockery, hand-painted trays, lacquered miniature boxes and brooches from Palekh, 'matryoshka' dolls, jewellery and pretty headscarves. Payment in these shops, as in all others, can be made only in roubles. Your hard currency can be easily changed at any of the numerous exchange points, some of which are located in the shops themselves.

However, by far the widest selection of traditional Russian souvenirs and the best bargains are to be found in street art markets such as the one on the Арбат (*arbat*), or at Вернисаж (*vyerneesazh*) in Moscow. Quality and prices vary, but haggling is acceptable practice here. It is not recommended that food such as caviar be bought here since it may not always be the genuine article.

Two shopping malls well worth a visit are ГУМ (*goom*; the letters stand for 'State Universal Shop') opposite the Kremlin, and Петровский Пассаж (*petrovskee passazh*), just a couple of minutes' walk from the Bolshoi Theatre.

Another shop which should not be left off your itinerary is the 'Елисеевский' (*yeleesye-evskee*) food shop, on Moscow's Tverskaya Street, and its twin on St. Petersburg's Nevsky Prospekt. Despite being rather neglected by time both shops remain striking examples of Russia's pre-revolutionary style.

More ambitious shoppers may be delighted to discover that works of art and antiques can sometimes be sold very unceremoniously and at relatively low prices. Before you buy, make enquiries to ensure you will not be disappointed as, without a receipt from a *beryozka* or official permission from the Ministry of Culture to take any work of art out of the country, there is a risk the item will be confiscated from you at the airport.

USEFUL WORDS AND PHRASES

baker	булочная	*boolachna-ya*
bookshop	книжный магазин	*kneezhni magazeen*
bookshop (*second-hand*)	букинистический магазин	*bookeeneesteechy-eskee magazeen*
butcher	мясо (*literally meat*)	*myasa*
to buy	купить	*koopeet'*
cake shop	кондитерская	*kandeetyerska-ya*
cheap	дешёвый (*m*)	*dyeshyovi*
	дешёвая (*f*)	*dyeshyova-ya*
	дешёвое (*n*)	*dyeshyova-ye*
chemist	аптека	*aptyeka*
department store	универмаг	*ooneevyermag*
fashion	мода	*moda*
fishmonger	рыба (*literally fish*)	*riba*
florist	цветы (*literally flowers*)	*tsvyeti*
foodstore	гастроном	*gastranom*
grocer	бакалея (*literally groceries*)	*bakalye-ya*
market	рынок	*rinak*
menswear	мужская одежда	*mooshska-ya adyezhda*
newspaper stand	газетный киоск	*gazyetni kee-osk*
receipt	чек	*chyek*
record shop	грампластинки (*literally records*)	*gramplasteenkee*
shoe repairs	ремонт обуви	*ryemont oboovee*
shoe shop	обувь (*literally footwear*)	*oboof*
shop	магазин	*magazeen*
to go shopping	ходить по магазинам	*khadeet' po mogazeenam*
souvenir shop	сувениры (*literally souvenirs*)	*soovyeneeri*
to spend	тратить	*trateet'*

stationer	канцтовары	*kantstavari*
supermarket	универсам	*ooneevyersam*
till	касса	*kasa*
toy shop	игрушки (*literally toys*)	*eegrooshkee*
women's wear	женская одежда	*zhenska-ya adyezhda*

I'd like …
Я хочу …
ya khachoo

Do you have …?
У вас есть …?
oo vas yest'

How much is this?
Сколько это стоит?
skol'ka eta stoeet

Where is the … department?
Где отдел …?
gd-ye atdyel

Do you have any more of these?
У вас есть ещё?
oo vas yest' yeshshyo

I'd like to change this, please
Будьте добры, я хочу это поменять
bood't-ye dabri, ya khachoo eta pamyenyat'

Have you anything cheaper?
У вас есть что-нибудь дешевле?
oo vas yest' shto-neeboot' dyeshevl-ye

Have you anything larger?
У вас есть что-нибудь побольше?
oo vas yest' shto-neeboot' pabol'shye

Have you anything smaller?
У вас есть что-нибудь поменьше?
oo vos yest' shto-neeboot' pamyen'shye

Do you have it in other colours?
У вас есть это другого цвета?
oo vas yest' eto droogova tsvyeta

Could you wrap it for me, please?
Заверните, пожалуйста
zavyerneet-ye, pazhalsta

Can I have a receipt?
Дайте, пожалуйста, чек
dIt-ye, pazhalsta chyek

Can I have a bag, please?
Дайте, пожалуйста, пакет
dIt-ye, pazhalsta pakyet

Can I try it (them) on?
Можно померять?
mozhna pamyeryat'

Where do I pay?
где платить?
gdye plateet'

Can I have a refund?
Я хочу получить обратно деньги
ya khachoo paloocheet' abratna dyen'gee

I'm just looking
Я просто смотрю
ya prosta smatryoo

I'll come back later
Я вернусь позже
ya vyernoos' pozhe

THINGS YOU'LL SEE

бакалея	*bakalye-ya*	groceries
букинистический магазин	*bookeeneesteechy-eskee magazeen*	second-hand bookshop
булочная	*boolachna-ya*	bakery
бытовая химия	*bitova-ya kheemee-ya*	household cleaning materials
верхний этаж	*vyerkhnee etash*	upper floor
возьмите тележку/ корзину	*vazmeet-ye tyelyeshkoo/ karzeenoo*	please take a trolley/basket
женская одежда	*zhenska-ya adyezhda*	women's clothing
игрушки	*eegrooshkee*	toys
канцтовары	*kantstavari*	stationer
касса	*kasa*	cash desk, till
книги	*kneegee*	bookshop
количество	*kaleechyestva*	quantity
кондитерская	*kandeetyerska-ya*	cake shop
меха	*myekha*	fur shop
мода	*moda*	fashion
мороженое	*marozhena-ye*	ice cream shop
мужская одежда	*mooshska-ya adyezhda*	menswear
мясо	*myasa*	butcher

→

не трогать	*nye trogat'*	please do not touch
обувь	*oboof*	shoe shop
овощи	*ovashee*	vegetables
отдел	*atdyel*	department
первый этаж	*pyervi etash*	ground floor
прокат	*prakat*	rental
самообслужи-вание	*samo-obsloozhee-vaneeye*	self-service
табак	*tabak*	tobacconist
универмаг	*ooneevyermag*	department store
цветы	*tsvyeti*	flowers
цена	*tsyena*	price

THINGS YOU'LL HEAR

oo vas yest' myelach?
Do you have any smaller money?

eezveneet-ye oo nas etava paka nyet
We're out of stock

eta vsyo, shto oo nas yest'
This is all we have

shto-neeboot' yeshyo?
Will there be anything else?

AT THE HAIRDRESSER

Useful Words and Phrases

appointment	запись	*zapees'*
beard	борода	*barada*
blond man/ woman	блондин/ блондинка	*blandeen/ blandeenka*
brush	щётка	*shshyotka*
comb	расчёска	*raschyoska*
curlers	бигуди	*beegoodee*
curly	кудрявый	*koodryavi*
dark	тёмный	*tyomni*
fringe	чёлка	*chyolka*
gel	гель для волос	*gyel dlya valos*
hair	волосы	*volasi*
haircut	стрижка	*streeshka*
hairdresser	парикмахер	*pareekmakhyer*
hairdryer	фен	*fyen*
hair spray	лак для волос	*lak dlya valos*
long hair	длинные волосы	*dleeniye volasi*
moustache	усы	*oosi*
parting	пробор	*prabor*
perm	перманент	*pyermanyent*
shampoo	шампунь	*shampoon'*
shaving foam	крем для бритья	*kryem dlya breet'ya*
short hair	короткие волосы	*karotkeeye volasi*
wavy hair	вьющиеся волосы	*v'yooshshee-yesa volasi*

I'd like to make an appointment
Я хочу записаться
ya khachoo zapeesat'sa

Just a trim, please
Немного подстигите, пожалуйста
nyemnoga padstreegeet-ye, pazhalsta

Not too much off
Много не снимайте
mnoga nye sneemlt-ye

A bit more off here, please
Покороче здесь, пожалуйста
pakaroch-ye zdyes', pazhalsta

I'd like a cut and blow-dry
Подстригите и сделайте укладку феном
padstreegeet-ye ee zdyellt-ye ooklatkoo fyenam

I'd like a perm
Я хочу перманент
ya khachoo pyermanyent

I don't want any hair spray
Лака не нужно
laka nye noozhna

THINGS YOU'LL SEE

женский зал	*zhenskee zal*	women's salon
краска для волос	*kraska dlya valos*	tint
мастер	*mastyer*	hairdresser
мужской зал	*mooshskoy zal*	men's hairdresser
парикмахер	*pareekmakhyer*	hairdresser
парикмахерская	*pareekmakherska-ya*	hairdresser's
перманент	*pyermanyent*	perm
сухой	*sookhoy*	dry
укладка	*ooklatka*	set
уложить волосы	*oolazheet' volasi*	to blow dry
феном	*fyenam*	

THINGS YOU'LL HEAR

shto vi khateet-ye?
How would you like it?

eta dastatachna koratka?
Is that short enough?

pakrit' lakam?
Would you like any hair spray?

SPORT

Active involvement by tourists in sport in Russia is most likely
to mean swimming, skating or skiing. Ask your hotel
information service for fuller details of how and where to do
what you want. Cross-country skiing is popular and skis for
this may be hired (eg at Sokolneekee Park in Moscow) or even
bought with relative ease. If you go anywhere off the beaten
track, make sure that you are with local people who know
what they are doing. Downhill skiing is becoming a popular
tourist attraction in the Caucacus, but skiers should not expect
it to be like Verbiers or Val d'Isère. You should check well in
advance with the tour organiser what you may need to bring
yourself, rather than assume that skiing equipment will be
available on site.

The Black Sea resorts are excellent for swimming, and
swimming pools can be found in Moscow, St Petersburg and
the larger towns.

Full details of current sporting events for spectators can be
obtained by asking your hotel information desk. Sportsmen
and women undertaking any activity outdoors in a Russian
winter should be very wary of the cold – it can be ferocious.

USEFUL WORDS AND PHRASES

athletics	атлетика	*atlyeteeka*
badminton	бадминтон	*badmeenton*
ball	мяч	*myach*
beach	пляж	*plyash*
bicycle	велосипед	*vyelaseepyet*
canoe	каноэ	*kanoe*
chess	шахматы	*shakhmati*
cross-country skiing	лыжный спорт	*lizhni sport*
cross-country skis	лыжи	*lizhee*
deck chair	шезлонг	*shezlonk*

downhill skiing	горнолыжный спорт	*garna-lizhni sport*
downhill skis	горные лыжи	*gorniye lizhee*
fishing	рыболовство	*ribalofstva*
fishing rod	удочка	*oodachka*
flippers	ласты	*lasti*
football (*sport*)	футбол	*footbol*
football (*ball*)	футбольный мяч	*footbol'ni myach*
football match	футбольный матч	*footbol'ni match*
goggles	защитные очки	*zasheetniye achkee*
gymnastics	гимнастика	*geemnasteeka*
harpoon	гарпун	*garpoon*
hockey	хоккей	*khakkay*
jogging	бег трусцой	*byeg troostsoy*
lake	озеро	*ozyera*
life jacket	спасательный жилет	*spasatyel'ni zheelyet*
lifeguard	спасатель	*spasatyel'*
mountaineering	альпинизм	*al'peeneezm*
oxygen bottles	кислородные баллоны	*keeslarodniye baloni*
pedal boat	водный велосипед	*vodni vyelaseepyet*
racket	ракетка	*rakyetka*
riding	верховая езда	*vyerkhava-ya yezda*
rowing boat	вёсельная лодка	*vyosyel'na-ya lotka*
to run	бегать	*byegat'*
sailing	парусный спорт	*paroosni sport*
sand	песок	*pyesok*
sea	море	*mor-ye*
to skate	кататься на коньках	*katatsa na kan'kakh*
skates	коньки	*kan'kee*
skating rink	каток	*katok*
to ski	кататься на лыжах	*katatsa na lizhakh*
skin diving	подводное плавание	*padvodna-ye plavaneeye*

stadium	стадион	*stadee-on*
sunshade	солнечный зонт	*solnyechni zont*
to swim	плавать	*plavat'*
swimming pool	бассейн	*basyeyn*
table tennis	настольный теннис	*nastolni tyenees*
tennis	теннис	*tyenees*
tennis court	теннисный корт	*tyeneesni kort*
tennis racket	теннисная ракетка	*tyeneesna-ya rakyetka*
volleyball	волейбол	*valyaybol*
walking	ходьба	*khad'ba*
water-skiing	воднолыжный спорт	*vadna-lizhni sport*
water-skis	водные лыжи	*vodniye lizhee*
wave	волна	*valna*
wet suit	плавательный костюм	*plavatyel'ni kastyoom*
windsurfing board	доска для сёрфинга	*daska dlya syorfeenga*
yacht	яхта	*yakhta*

How do I get to the beach?
Как попасть на пляж?
kak papast' na plyash

How deep is the water here?
Какая глубина воды здесь?
kaka-ya gloobeena vadi zdyes'

Is there an outdoor pool here?
Здесь есть открытый бассейн?
zdyes' yest' atkriti basyeyn

Can I swim here?
Здесь можно плавать?
zdyes' mozhna plavat'

Can I fish here?
Здесь можно ловить рыбу?
zdyes' mozhna laveet' riby

Do I need a licence?
Мне нужно разрешение?
mnye noozhna razryesh_eneeye

I would like to hire a sunshade
Можно взять напрокат зонтик?
mozhna vzyat' naprakat zonteek

How much does it cost per hour?
Сколько это стоит в час?
skol'ka eta sto-eet fchas

I would like to take water-skiing lessons
Я хочу брать уроки катания на водных лыжах
ya khachoo brat' oorokee kataneeya na vodnikh lizhakh

Where can I hire ...?
Где можно взять напрокат ...?
gdye mozhno vsyat' naprakat

THINGS YOU'LL SEE

билеты	*beelyeti*	tickets
велосипедная трасса	*vyelaseepyedna-ya trasa*	cycle path
велосипеды	*vyelaseepyedi*	bicycles
водные виды	*vodniye veedi*	water sports

спорта	*sporta*	
горные лыжи	*gorniye lizhee*	downhill skis
коньки	*kan'kee*	skates
лыжи	*lizhee*	cross-country skis
напрокат	*naprakat*	for hire
не нырять	*nye niryat'*	no diving
парусные лодки	*paroosniye lotkee*	sailing boats
первая помощь	*pyerva-ya pomashsh'*	first aid
плавать запрещается	*plavat' zapryeshshа-yetsa*	no swimming
пляж	*plyash*	beach
порт	*port*	port
рыбная ловля запрещена	*ribna-ya lovlya zapryeshyena*	no fishing
спортивное оборудование	*sparteevna-ye abaroodavaneeye*	sporting facilities
спортивный центр	*sparteevni tsyentr*	sports centre
спасательный жилет	*spasatyel'ni zheelyet*	life jacket
спасатель	*spasatel'*	lifeguard
стадион	*stadee-on*	stadium
уроки по водным лыжам	*oorokee pa vodnim lizham*	water-skiing lessons
футбольное поле	*footbol'na-ye pol-ye*	football pitch

POST OFFICES AND BANKS

As far as postage is concerned, it is easier to use the facilities at your hotel, if these are available, rather than go to a post office. You will thus avoid long queues and will be able to deal with people who are used to foreigners. You will not have to suffer the more exasperating features of the postal service, such as arbitrary closing or having no stamps. For airmail letters use a международный конверт (*mezhdoonarodni kanvyert*), or international envelope, and allow an average of two weeks for arrival. Postcards, stamps and envelopes can be purchased at newspaper kiosks and post offices. Postboxes are blue; in Moscow, those painted red are for local (city) mail only.

Most large towns and cities now boast a multitude of exchange bureaux and banks where you can change hard currency for roubles and vice versa – rates do not usually vary sufficiently from bank to bank to merit shopping around.

Although customs currency checks have relaxed in recent years it is still advisable to get and retain exchange receipts. These will account for expenditures of the currency you declared on your currency declaration form when you entered the country.

It should be noted that the rouble is now the only legal form of tender in Russian shops and restaurants. Hard currency is no longer accepted in its cash form, although a growing number of outlets do take credit cards. Your hard currency can be easily changed at exchange points, some of which will be located in the shops themselves. Rates offered in the latter, however, tend to be worse than in the banks and independent exchange bureaux.

USEFUL WORDS AND PHRASES

airmail	авиапочта	*avee-yapochta*
bank	банк	*bank*
banknote	банкнота	*banknota*
to change	обменять	*abmyenyat'*
cheque	чек	*chyek*
collection	выемка	*vi-yemka*
counter	стойка	*stoyka*
customs form	таможенная декларация	*tamozhena-ya dyeklaratsee-ya*
delivery	доставка	*dastafka*
dollar	доллар	*dolar*
exchange rate	обменный курс	*abmyeni koors*
form	бланк	*blank*
international money order	поручение на международный перевод	*poruchyeneeye na myezhdoo-narodni pyeryevot*
letter	письмо	*pees'mo*
letter box	почтовый ящик	*pachtovi yashsheek*
parcel	посылка	*pasilka*
post	почта	*pochta*
postage rates	почтовые тарифы	*pachtoviye tareefi*
postcard	открытка	*atkritka*
postcode	почтовый индекс	*pachtovi eendyeks*
poste restante	почта до востребования	*pochta da-vastryebavanee-ya*
postman	почтальон	*pachtal'on*
post office	почта	*pochta*
pound sterling	фунт стерлингов	*foont styerleengaf*
registered letter	заказное письмо	*zakazno-ye pees'mo*
stamp	марка	*marka*
traveller's cheque	дорожный чек	*darozhni chyek*

How much is a postcard to …?
Сколько стоит отправить открытку в ...?
skol'ka sto-eet atpraveet' atkritkoo v

I want to register this letter
Я хочу отправить заказное письмо
ya khachoo atpraveet' zakazno-ye pees'mo

I want to send this letter to …
Я хочу отправить это письмо в ...
ya khachoo atpraveet' eta pees'mo v

By airmail, please
Авиапочтой, пожалуйста
avee-apochtay, pazhalsta

How long does the post to … take?
Сколько это будет идти до ...?
skol'ka eta boodyet eetee do

Where can I post this?
Где я могу это отправить?
gdye ya magoo eta atpraveet'

Is there any mail for me?
Есть письма для меня?
yest' pees'ma dlya myenya

My last name is …
Моя фамилия ...
ma-ya fameelee-ya

I'd like to send a fax
Я хочу отправить факс
ya khachoo atpraveet' faks

I'd like to change this into …
Я хочу разменять это на ...
ya khach<u>oo</u> razmyenyat'<u>e</u>ta na

Can I cash these traveller's cheques?
Можно обменять эти дорожные чеки?
m<u>o</u>zhna abmyen<u>ya</u>t' <u>e</u>tee dar<u>o</u>zhniye ch<u>ye</u>kee

What is the exchange rate for the pound/dollar?
Какой курс обмена фунтов стерлингов/долларов?
kak<u>oy</u> koors abm<u>ye</u>na f<u>oo</u>ntaf st<u>ye</u>rleengaf/d<u>o</u>laraf

---

THINGS YOU'LL SEE

авиапочта	*avee-yap<u>o</u>chta*	airmail
адрес	*<u>a</u>dryes*	address
адресат	*adryes<u>a</u>t*	addressee
банк	*bank*	bank
денежные переводы	*d<u>ye</u>nyezhniye pyeryev<u>o</u>di*	money orders
заказные письма	*zakazniye p<u>ee</u>s'ma*	registered mail
заполнить	*zap<u>o</u>lneet'*	to fill in
касса	*k<u>a</u>sa*	cash desk
марка	*m<u>a</u>rka*	stamp
марки	*m<u>a</u>rkee*	stamps
обмен валюты	*abm<u>ye</u>n val<u>yoo</u>ti*	currency exchange
открытка	*atkr<u>i</u>tka*	postcard
отправитель	*atprav<u>ee</u>tyel'*	sender
пакет	*pak<u>ye</u>t*	packet
письмо	*pees'm<u>o</u>*	letter
почта	*p<u>o</u>chta*	letter box; post office
почта до востребования	*p<u>o</u>chta da vastr<u>ye</u>bavanee-ya*	poste restante
почтовый индекс	*pacht<u>o</u>vi <u>ee</u>ndyeks*	postcode

→

приём посылок	*pree-yom pasilak*	parcels counter
стоимость международной отправки	*sto-eemast' myezhdoonarodnay atpravkee*	postage abroad
тариф	*tareef*	charge
телеграммы	*tyelyegrami*	telegrams
часы работы	*chasi raboti*	opening hours

COMMUNICATIONS

Telephones: You can make both international and local calls from your hotel. Most hotels in the big cities have international phone booths or satellite phone facilities. These booths take phonecards which can normally be bought from your hotel reception, as well as several major credit cards. You will also find payphones on the street, at stations, restaurants, etc.

If you do not have access to an international direct-dial phone, then your call must be booked through the operator. Although essential phrases are included below, the operators connecting you will normally speak English. If you are unable to call from a hotel, you can go to a telephone office to make the call from there.

USEFUL WORDS AND PHRASES

ambulance	скорая помощь (03)	*skora-ya pomashsh'*
call	звонок	*zvanok*
to call	звонить	*zvaneet'*
code	код	*kod*
to dial	набирать номер	*nabeerat' nomyer*
dialling tone	гудок	*goodok*
email	е-мэйл	*ee-mayl*
enquiries	справочная (09)	*spravachna-ya*
extension (*number*)	добавочный (номер)	*dabavachni (nomyer)*
fax machine	факс	*faks*
fire	пожар (01)	*pazhar*
international call	международный звонок	*myezhdoo-narodni zvanok*
mobile phone	мобильный телефон	*mobeel'niy tyelyefon*
number	номер	*nomyer*
payphone	телефон-автомат	*tyelyefon-aftamat*
phonecard	телефонная карточка	*tyelyefonaya kartachka*

police	милиция (02)	*meeleetsee-ya*
receiver	(телефонная) трубка	*(tyelyefona-ya) troopka*
telephone	телефон	*tyelyefon*
telephone box	телефон-автомат	*tyelyefon-aftamat*
telephone directory	телефонный справочник	*tyelyefoni spravachneek*
wrong number	неправильный номер	*nyepraveel'ni nomyer*

Where is the nearest phone box?
Где ближайший телефон-автомат?
gdye bleezhIshee tyelyefon-aftamat

Is there a telephone directory?
У вас есть телефонный справочник?
oo vas yest' tyelyefoni spravachneek

I would like the directory for…
Мне нужен телефонный справочник для…
mnye noozhen tyelyefoni spravachneek dlya

I would like to order a call to London for 8 o'clock tomorrow evening
Я хочу заказать разговор с Лондоном на восемь вечера завтра
ya khachoo zakazat' razgavor slondanam na vosyem' vyechyera zaftra

Can I call abroad from here?
Можно позвонить за границу отсюда?
mozhna pazvaneet' zagraneetsoo atsyooda

How much is a call to…?
Сколько стоит звонок в…?
skol'ka stoeet zvanok v

I would like a number in …
Мне нужен номер в ...
mnye noozhen nomyer v

Hello, this is … speaking
Алло, говорит ...
allo, gavareet

Is that …?
Это ...?
eta

Speaking *(literally: I'm listening)*
Слушаю
sloosha-yoo

I would like to speak to …
Позовите, пожалуйста ...
pazaveet-ye pazhalsta …

Extension …, please
Добавочный ..., пожалуйста
dabavachni …, pazhalsta

Please say that he/she called
Пожалуйста, передайте, что звонил *(m)*/звонила *(f)*
pazhalsta pyeryedIt-ye shto zvaneel/zvaneela

Ask him/her to call me back, please
Попросите его/её позвонить мне, пожалуйста
papraseet-ye yevo/yeyo pazvaneet' mnye pazhalsta

My number is …
Мой номер ...
moy nomyer …

Do you know where he/she is?
Вы знаете, где он/она?
vi znayet-ye gdye on/ana

When will he/she be back?
Когда он/она вернётся?
kagda on/ana vyernyotsa

Could you leave him/her a message?
Вы можете передать ему/ей?
vi mozhet-ye pyeryedat' yemoo/yay

I'll ring back later
Я позвоню позже
ya pazvanyoo pozhe

What's your fax number/email address?
Какой у вас номер факса/адрес электронной почты?
kakoy oovas nomyer faksa/adiyes elyektronay pochti

Did you get my fax/email?
Вы получили мой факс/е-мэйл?
vi paloocheelee moy faks/ee-mayl

Please resend your fax
Пожалуйста, перешлите факс еще раз
pazhalste pyereeshleetye vash faks yesho

Can I send an email/fax from here?
Можно отсюда отправить е-мэйл/факс?
mozhna atsyyooda atpraveet ee-mayl/fax

Can I use the photocopier/fax machine?
Можно воспользоваться ксероксом/факсом?
mozhna vaspol'zavatsa ksyeraksam/faksam

THINGS YOU'LL SEE

автоматический набор	*avtomateechyeskeey nabor*	direct dialling
код	*kot*	code
междугородный звонок	*myezhdoo-garodnee zvanok*	long-distance call
местный звонок	*myestni zvanok*	local call
не работает	*nye rabota-yet*	out of order
справочная	*spravachna-ya*	enquiries
стоимость	*sto-eemast'*	charges

THINGS YOU'LL HEAR

skyem vi khateet-ye gavareet'?
Who would you like to speak to?

vi nye tooda papalee
You've got the wrong number

kto gavareet?
Who's speaking?

kakoy oo vas nomyer?
What is your number?

eezveeneet-ye yevo/yeyo nyet
Sorry, he/she's not in

on/ana vernyotsa v …
He/she'll be back at … o'clock

pyeryezvaneet-ye pazhalsta zaftra
Please call again tomorrow

ya pyeryedam shto vi zvaneelee
I'll say that you called

HEALTH

If you fall seriously ill during your visit to Russia, notify the hotel management as most major hotels have their own doctor. Sometimes the Russian doctor treating you will speak English, but you may find an interpreter useful.

There are some medical services, such as the European Medical Centre in Moscow, that deal with foreigners but they can be expensive.

If you need immediate attention, and have no time to contact a doctor, go straight to the nearest casualty department.

All travellers to Russia should make sure they have adequate medical insurance as local healthcare is not of a very good standard and charges for private services can be very high.

For minor ailments you can go to a chemist (аптека *aptyeka*). These can be identified by a green cross hanging outside. The pharmacist can often suggest a Russian alternative if you tell them what drug you are looking for.

Moscow has a number of all-night pharmacies.

USEFUL WORDS AND PHRASES

accident	несчастный случай	*nyeshastni sloochI*
ambulance	скорая помощь	*skora-ya pomashsh'*
appendicitis	аппендицит	*apyendeetseet*
appendix	аппендикс	*apyendeeks*
aspirin	аспирин	*aspeereen*
asthma	астма	*astma*
backache	боль в спине	*bol' vspeenye*
bandage	бинт	*beent*
bite (*by dog*)	укус (собаки)	*ookoos (sabakee)*
bite (*by insect*)	укус (насекомого)	*ookoos (nasyekomava)*
bladder	мочевой пузырь	*machyevoy poozir'*
blister	волдырь	*valdir'*
blood	кровь	*krof'*

burn (*noun*)	ожог	*azhok*
cancer	рак	*rak*
chemist	аптека	*aptyeka*
chest	грудь	*groot'*
chickenpox	ветрянка	*vyetryanka*
cold (*noun*)	простуда	*prastooda*
concussion	контузия	*kantoozee-ya*
constipation	запор	*zapor*
contact lenses	контактные линзы	*kantaktniye leenzi*
corn	мозоль	*mazol'*
cough (*noun*)	кашель	*kashel'*
cut	порез	*paryes*
dentist	зубной врач	*zoobnoy vrach*
diabetes	диабет	*dee-abyet*
diarrhoea	понос	*panos*
dizziness	головокружение	*galava-kroozhgneeye*
doctor (*profession*)	врач	*vrach*
doctor (*as form of address*)	доктор	*doktar*
earache	боль в ухе	*bol' vookh-ye*
fever	температура	*tyempyeratoora*
filling	пломба	*plomba*
first aid	первая помощь	*pyerva-ya pomashsh'*
flu	грипп	*greep*
fracture	перелом	*pyeryelom*
German measles	краснуха	*krasnookha*
glasses	очки	*achkee*
gum	десна	*dyesna*
haemorrhage	кровотечение	*kravatyechyeneeye*
hay fever	сенная лихорадка	*syennaya leekharadka*
headache	головная боль	*galavna-ya bol'*
heart	сердце	*syertse*
heart attack	сердечный приступ	*syerdyechni preestoop*

hepatitis	гепатит	*gyepateet*
HIV positive	ВИЧ-инфици-рованный	*veech-een feetsiravaniy*
hospital	больница	*bal'-neetsa*
ill	болен *(m)*/больна *(f)*	*bolyen/bal'na*
indigestion	несварение	*nyesvaryeneeye*
infected	заражённый	*zarazhyoni*
injection	укол	*ookol*
itch	зуд	*zoot*
kidney	почка	*pochka*
lump	опухоль	*opookhal'*
measles	корь	*kor'*
migraine	мигрень	*meegryen'*
mumps	свинка	*sveenka*
nausea	тошнота	*tashnata*
nurse	медсестра	*myedsyestra*
operation	операция	*apyeratsee-ya*
optician	окулист	*akooleest*
pain	боль	*bol'*
penicillin	пенициллин	*pyeneetseeleen*
plaster *(sticky)*	пластырь	*plastir'*
plaster *(of Paris)*	гипс	*geeps*
pneumonia	пневмония	*pnyevmanee-ya*
pregnant	беременная	*byeryemyena-ya*
prescription	рецепт	*ryetsyept*
rheumatism	ревматизм	*ryevmateezm*
scratch	царапина	*tsarapeena*
sore throat	боль в горле	*bol' vgorl-ye*
splinter	заноза	*zanoza*
sprain	растяжение связок	*rastyazheneeye svyazak*
sting	укус	*ookoos*
stomach	желудок	*zheloodak*
temperature	температура	*tyempyeratoora*
tonsils	миндалины	*meendaleeni*

toothache	зубная боль	*zoobna-ya bol'*
ulcer	язва	*yazva*
vaccination	прививка	*preeveefka*
whooping cough	коклюш	*kaklyoosh*

I feel sick
Меня тошнит
myenya tashneet

I feel travel sick
Меня укачало
myenya ookachala

I have a pain in ...
У меня болит ...
oo myenya baleet

I do not feel well
Мне плохо
mnye plokha

I feel faint
Мне дурно
mnye doorna

I feel dizzy
У меня кружится голова
oo myenya kroozheetsa galava

It hurts here
Болит здесь
baleet zdyes'

It's a sharp pain
Острая боль
ostra-ya bol'

It's a dull pain
Тупая боль
toopa-ya bol'

It hurts all the time
Болит всё время
baleet vsyo vryemya

It only hurts now and then
Болит время от времени
baleet vryema at vryemyenee

It hurts when you touch it
Болит, когда вы трогаете
baleet kagda vi troga-yet-ye

It hurts more at night
Болит сильнее ночью
baleet seel'nyeye nochyoo

It stings
Жжёт
zhyot

It aches
Болит
baleet

I have a temperature
У меня температура
oo myenya tyempyeratoora

I'm ... months pregnant
Я на ... месяце беременности
ya na ... myesyatse beeryemyenastee

I need a prescription for …
Мне нужен рецепт для …
mnye noozhen ryetsyept dlya

Can you take these if you're pregnant/breastfeeding?
Это можно беременным/кормящим грудью?
eta mozhna b'eeryemyehim/karmyasheem grood'yoo

I normally take …
Обычно я принимаю …
bichna ya preeneema-yoo

I'm allergic to …
У меня аллергия на …
oo myenya allyergee-ya na

Have you got anything for …?
У вас есть что-нибудь от …?
oo vas yest' shto-neeboot' ot

Do I need a prescription for this?
Мне нужен рецепт для этого?
mnye noozhen ryetsyept dlya etava

I have lost a filling
У меня выпала пломба
oo myenya vipala plomba

THINGS YOU'LL SEE

больница	*bal'neetsa*	hospital
врач	*vrach*	doctor
дежурная аптека	*dyezhoorna-ya aptyeka*	duty chemist
зубной врач	*zoobnoy vrach*	dentist
клиника	*kleeneeka*	clinic
кровяное давление	*kravyano-ye davlyeneeye*	blood pressure
лекарство	*lyekarstva*	medicine
нарыв	*nariv*	abscess
натощак	*natashshak*	on an empty stomach
окулист	*akooleest*	optician
осмотр	*asmotr*	check-up
отолоринголог	*atalareengolak*	ear, nose and throat specialist
очки	*achkee*	glasses
пломба	*plomba*	filling
поликлиника	*paleekleeneeka*	surgery
пункт скорой помощи	*poonkt skoray pomashshee*	first-aid post
рентген	*ryentgyen*	X-ray
рецепт	*ryetsyept*	prescription
скорая помощь	*skora-ya pomash'*	ambulance
укол	*ookol*	injection

THINGS YOU'LL HEAR

preeneemIt-ye po ... tablyetkee
Take ... tablets at a time

svadoy
With water

razzhooyt-ye
Chew them

adeen raz/dva raza/tree raza vdyen'
Once/twice/three times a day

tol'ka pyeryed snom
Only when you go to bed

shto vi abichna preeneema-yet-ye?
What do you normally take?

vam noozhna pItee kvrachoo
I think you should see a doctor

eezveeneet-ye oo nas etava nyet
I'm sorry, we don't have that

dlya etava vam noozhen ryetsyept
For that you need a prescription

MINI-DICTIONARY

about: about 16 okala shesnatsatee
accident avaree-ya
accommodation razmyeshshyeneeye
ache bol'
adaptor transfarmatar
address adryes
admission charge plata za fkhot
after posl-ye
aftershave adyekalon
again snova
against proteef
air conditioning kandeetsee-anyer
aircraft samalyot
air hostess styoo-ardyesa
airline avee-aleenee-ya
airport aeraport
alarm clock boodeel'neek
alcohol alkagol'
all vyes'
   all the streets fsye ooleetsi
   that's all, thanks fsyo, spaseeba
almost pachtee
alone adeen
already oozhe
always fsyegda
ambulance skora-ya pomashsh'
America amyereeka
American amyereekanskee
   (man) amyereekanyets
   (female) amyereekanka
and ee
ankle ladishka
anorak koortka
another: another room droogoy nomyer
   another coffee yeshyo kof-ye
answering machine afta-atvyetcheek
antifreeze anteefreez

antique shop anteekvarni magazeen
apartment kvarteera
aperitif apyereeteef
appetite apyeteet
apple yablaka
application form blank
appointment zapees'
apricot abreekos
arm rooka
art eeskoostva
art gallery khoodozhestvena-ya galyerya-ya
artist khoodozhneek
as: as soon as possible kak mozhna skarye-ye
ashtray pyepyel'neetsa
aspirin aspeergen
at: at the post office na pocht-ye
   at night noch'yoo
   at 3 o'clock ftree chasa
attractive preevlyekatyel'ni
aunt tyotya
Australia afstralee-ya
Australian afstraleeskee
   (man) afstraleeyets
   (woman) afstraleeka
automatic afta-mateechyeskee
away: is it far away? eta dalyeko?
   go away! ookhadeet-ye
awful oozhasni
axe tapor

baby ryebyonak
baby wipes slyoonyatcheekee
back *(not front)* nazat
   (body) speena
bad plakhoy

bakery b<u>oo</u>lachna-ya
balalaika balal<u>l</u>ka
balcony balk<u>o</u>n
ball myach
ballet bal<u>ye</u>t
ball-point pen sh<u>a</u>reekava-ya
  r<u>oo</u>chka
Baltic (*states*) preeb<u>a</u>lteeka
banana ban<u>a</u>n
band (*musicians*) ark<u>ye</u>str
bandage beent
bank bank
banknote bankn<u>o</u>ta
bar bar
  bar of chocolate pl<u>ee</u>tka shakal<u>a</u>da
barber's pareekhm<u>a</u>khyerska-ya
basement padv<u>a</u>l
basin (*sink*) r<u>a</u>kaveena
basket karz<u>ee</u>na
bath v<u>a</u>na
  to have a bath
  preeneem<u>a</u>t' van<u>oo</u>
bathroom v<u>a</u>na-ya
battery batar<u>ay</u>ka
beach plyash
beans fas<u>o</u>l'
beard barad<u>a</u>
because patam<u>oo</u> shto
bed krav<u>a</u>t'
bed linen pasty<u>e</u>l'na-ye byel'<u>yo</u>
bedroom sp<u>a</u>l'nya
beef gav<u>ya</u>deena
beer p<u>ee</u>va
before do
beginner nacheen<u>a</u>-yooshee
behind za
beige by<u>e</u>zhevi
bell (*church*) k<u>o</u>lakal
  (*door*) zvan<u>o</u>k
Belorussia byelar<u>oo</u>see-ya
below pod
belt p<u>o</u>-yas
beside <u>o</u>kala

best l<u>oo</u>chee
better l<u>oo</u>che
between my<u>e</u>zhdoo
bicycle vyelaseep<u>ye</u>d
big bal'sh<u>oy</u>
bikini koop<u>a</u>l'neek
bill shyot
bird pt<u>ee</u>tsa
birthday dyen' razhd<u>ye</u>nee-ya
  happy birthday!
  zdny<u>o</u>m razhd<u>ye</u>nee-ya
biscuit pyechy<u>e</u>n'ye
bite (*verb*) koos<u>a</u>t'
  (*noun*) ook<u>oo</u>s
  (*by insect*) nasyek<u>o</u>mava
bitter g<u>o</u>r'kee
black chy<u>o</u>rni
blackcurrant chy<u>o</u>rna-ya smar<u>o</u>deena
Black Sea chy<u>o</u>rna-ye m<u>o</u>r-ye
blanket ady<u>e</u>yala
bleach (*verb: hair*) v<u>i</u>svyetleet'
blind (*cannot see*) slyep<u>oy</u>
blister v<u>a</u>ldir
blood krof'
blouse bl<u>oo</u>ska
blue s<u>ee</u>nee
boat parakh<u>o</u>t
  (*smaller*) l<u>o</u>tka
body ty<u>e</u>la
bolt (*on door*) bolt
bone kost'
bonnet (*car*) kap<u>o</u>t
book (*noun*) kn<u>ee</u>ga
  (*verb*) zak<u>a</u>zivat'
booking office k<u>a</u>sa
bookshop kn<u>ee</u>zhni magaz<u>ee</u>n
boot (*car*) bag<u>a</u>shneek
  (*footwear*) sap<u>o</u>g
border gran<u>ee</u>tsa
boring sk<u>oo</u>shni
born: I was born in …
  (*male*) ya rad<u>ee</u>lsa v …
  (*female*) ya rad<u>ee</u>las' v …

both _o_ba
  both of them an_ee_ _o_ba
  both of us mi _o_ba
  both … and … ee … ee …
bottle boot_i_lka
bottle opener sht_o_par
bottom dno
bowl p_ee_dala
box kar_o_pka
boy m_a_l'cheek
boyfriend drook
bra byoostg_a_l'tyer
bracelet brasl_y_et
brandy kan'y_a_k
bread khlyep
break (_noun_) pyery_e_rif
  (_verb_) lam_a_t'
breakdown (_car_) pal_o_mka
  (_nervous_) ny_e_rvna-ye
  rastr_o_ystva
breakfast z_a_ftrak
breathe dish_a_t'
  I can't breathe
  mnye tr_oo_dna dish_a_t'
bridge most
briefcase partf_y_el'
British breet_a_nskee
brochure brashy_oo_ra
broken sl_o_mani
  broken leg
  sl_o_mana-ya naga
brooch brosh
brother brat
brown kar_ee_chnyevi
bruise seeny_a_k
brush (_noun_) shy_o_tka
  (_paint_) keest'
bucket vyedr_o_
building zd_a_neeye
Bulgarian balg_a_rskee
burglar vor
burn (_verb_) abzheeg_a_t'
  (_noun_) azh_o_k

bus aft_o_boos
bus station aft_o_boosna-ya st_a_ntsee-ya
business d_y_ela
  it's none of your business
  _e_ta nye v_a_she d_y_ela
busy (_occupied_) z_a_nyat
but no
butcher myasn_o_y magaz_ee_n
butter m_a_sla
button p_oo_gaveetsa
buy pakoop_a_t'
by: by the window _o_kala akn_a_

cabbage kap_oo_sta
cable TV kabyel'naye tyelyeveedeeneeye
café kaf_e_
cake per_o_k
calculator kal'k_oo_lyatar
call (_summon_) zvat'
  (_telephone_) zvan_ee_t'
  what's it called? kak _e_ta naz_i_va-yetsa ?
camera fata-apar_a_t
campsite ky_e_mpeeng
can (_tin_) b_a_nka
can: can I have …? m_o_zhna …?
Canada kan_a_da
Canadian kan_a_tskee
  (_man_) kan_a_dyets
  (_female_) kan_a_tka
cancer rak
candle svy_e_cha
canoe kan_o_e
cap (_bottle_) pr_o_pka
  (_hat_) ky_e_pka
car mash_ee_na
caravan d_o_m-aftaf_oo_rgon
card atkr_i_tka
cardigan k_o_fta
careful ast_a_rozhni
  be careful! ast_a_rozhna!
carpet kavy_o_r
carriage (_train_) vag_o_n

carrot markof'
car seat *(for a baby)* dyetskaye seedyen
case chyemadan
cash naleechniye
  (coins) manyeti
  to pay cash plateet' naleechnimee
Caspian Sea kaspeeskaye mor-ye
cassette kasyeta
cassette player magneetafon
castle zamak
cat koshka
cathedral sabor
Caucasus kafkas
cauliflower tsvyetna-ya kapoosta
cave pyeshshyera
cemetery kladbeeshsh-ye
centre tsyentr
certificate oodastavyeryeneeye
chair stool
chambermaid gorneechna-ya
change *(noun: money)* abmyen
  (verb: clothes) pyerye-adyevat'sa
  (verb: money) razmyenyat'
cheap dyeshyovi
cheers! *(toast)* vashe zdarov'ye!
cheese sir
chemist *(shop)* aptyeka
cheque chyek
chequebook chyekava-ya kneeshka
cherry veeshnya
chess shakhmati
chest groot'
chewing gum zhevatyel'na-ya ryezeenka
chicken kooreetsa
child ryebyonak
children dyetee
China keetI
chips kartofyel' free
chocolate shakalat
  box of chocolates
  karopka shakaladnikh kanfyet
chop *(food)* atbeevna-ya
  (cut) roobeet'

church tserkaf'
cigar seegara
cigarette seegaryeta
cinema keeno
circus tseerk
city gorat
city centre tsyentr gorada
class klas
classical music
  klaseechyeska-ya moozika
clean cheesti
clear *(obvious)* yasni
  is that clear? eta yasna?
clever oomni
clock chasi
close *(near)* bleeskee
  (stuffy) dooshni
  (verb) zakrivat'
  the shop is closed
  magazeen zakrit
clothes adyezhda
club kloop
coach aftoboos
  (of train) vagon
coach station aftoboosna-ya stantsee-ya
coat pal'to
coat hanger vyeshalka
cockroach tarakan
coffee kof-ye
coin manyeta
cold *(illness)* greep
  (adj) khalodni
collar varatneek
collection *(stamps etc)* kalyektsee-ya
collective *(noun)* kalyekteef
colour tsvyet
colour film tsvyetna-ya plyonka
comb *(noun)* rashshyoska
  (verb) preechyosivat'sa
come preekhadeet'
  I come from … ya eez …
  come here! eedeet-ye syooda!
communication cord stop-kran

Communist Party
 kamooneesteechyeska-ya partee-ya
compartment koope
complicated slozhni
concert kantsyert
conductor (*bus*) kandooktar
 (*orchestra*) deereezhyor
congratulations! pazdravlya-yoo!
constipation zapor
consulate konsoolstva
contact lenses kantaktniye leenzi
contraceptive
 prateeva-zachatachna-ye sryedstva
cook (*noun*) povar
 (*verb*) gatoveet'
cooking utensils
 kookhaniye preenadlyezhnastee
cool prakhladni
cork propka
corkscrew shtopar
corner oogal
corridor kareedor
cosmetics kasmyeteeka
Cossack kazak
cost (*verb*) sto-eet'
 what does it cost?
 skol'ka eta sto-eet?
cotton khlopak
cotton wool vata
cough (*verb*) kashlyat'
 (*noun*) kashel'
country (*state*) strana
 (*not town*) dyeryevnya
course: of course kanyeshna
cousin (*male*) dvayooradni brat
 (*female*) dvayooradna-ya syestra
crab krap
cream sleefkee
credit card
 kryedeetna-ya kartachka
crew ekeepash
Crimea krim
crisps khroostyashee kartofyel'

crowded pyeryepolnyeni
cruise kroo-ees
crutches kastilee
cry (*weep*) plakat'
 (*shout*) kreechat'
cucumber agooryets
cuff links zapankee
cup chashka
cupboard shkaf
curtain zanavyeska
Customs tamozhnya
cut (*noun*) paryez
 (*verb*) ryezat'

dad papa
damp siroy
dance tanyets
dangerous apasni
dark tyomni
date cheeslo
daughter doch'
day dyen'
dead myortvi
deaf glookhoy
dear daragoy
deck chair shezlong
deep gloobokee
delay zadyershka
deliberately narochna
dentist zoobnoy vrach
dentures pratyez
deodorant dyezadarant
depart (*verb*) oo-yezhat'
department store ooneevyermak
develop (*a film*) pra-yavlyat'
diamond breelee-ant
diarrhoea panos
diary dnyevneek
dictionary slavar'
die oomeerat'
diesel deezyel
diet dee-yeta

different (*other*) droog_oy_
  (*various*) r_a_zni
  that's different _e_ta droog_o_-ye d_ye_la
difficult tr_oo_dni
dining room stal_o_va-ya
dinner ab_ye_t
directory (*telephone*)
  tyelyef_o_ni spr_a_vachneek
dirty gry_a_zni
disabled eenval_ee_t
disposable nappies adnar_a_zaviye
  peely_o_nkee
dive nir_ya_t'
diving board trampl_ee_n
divorced (*male*) razvyed_yo_ni
  (*female*) razvyeden_a_
do d_ye_lat'
doctor vrach
document dakoom_ye_nt
dog sab_a_ka
doll k_oo_kla
dollar d_o_lar
door dvyer'
double room n_o_myer sdvoospal'nay
  krav_a_t'yoo
down fnees
drawing pin kn_o_pka
dress pl_a_t'ye
drink (*verb*) peet'
  (*noun*) nap_ee_tak
drinking water peet'_ye_va-ya vad_a_
drive (*verb*) vad_ee_t'
driver vad_ee_tyel'
driving licence vad_ee_tyel'skeeye prav_a_
drunk p'_ya_ni
dry sookh_o_y
dry cleaner kheemch_ee_stka
dummy (*for baby*) s_o_ska
during va-vr_ye_mya
dustbin m_oo_sarni y_a_shsheek
duster tr_ya_pka dlya p_i_lee
duty-free byesp_o_shleena-ya targ_o_vlya

each (*every*) k_a_zhdi
  twenty roubles each
  dv_a_tsat' roobly_ay_ k_a_zhdi
ear _oo_kha
  (*plural*) _oo_shee
early r_a_na
earrings sy_e_r'gee
east vast_o_k
Easter p_a_skha
easy ly_o_khkee
eat yest'
egg ylts_o_
elastic ryez_ee_nka
elbow l_o_kat'
electric elyektr_ee_chyeskee
electricity elyektr_ee_chyestva
else: something else sht_o_-ta yeshshy_o_
  someone else kt_o_-ta yeshshy_o_
  somewhere else gd_ye_-ta yeshshy_o_
elevator leeft
email ee-m_a_yl
email address adr_y_es elekt_f_onay p_o_chti
embarrassed smooshy_o_ni
embassy pas_o_l'stva
emerald eez_oo_mr_oo_t
emergency exit zapasn_oy_ v_i_khat
empty poost_oy_
end kan_ye_ts
engaged (*couple*) pam_o_lvlyeni
  (*occupied*) z_a_nyat
engine (*motor*) dv_ee_gatyel'
England _a_nglee-ya
English angl_ee_skee
  (*language*) angl_ee_skee yaz_i_k
Englishman angleech_a_neen
Englishwoman angleech_a_nka
enlargement oovyeleech_ye_neeye
enough dast_a_tachna
enter fkhad_ee_t'
entertainment razvlyech_ye_neeye
entrance fkhot
envelope kanv_ye_rt
especially as_o_byena

Europe yevr**o**pa
evening v**ye**chyer
every k**a**zhdi
everyone fsye
everything fsyo
everywhere vyezd-**ye**
example preem**ye**r
  for example napreem**ye**r
excellent atl**ee**chni
excess baggage pyeryev**ye**s bagazh**a**
exchange *(verb)* myen**ya**t'
exchange rate val**yoo**tni koors
excursion eksk**oo**rsee-ya
excuse me! *(to get past)*
  eezveen**ee**t-ye!
  (to get attention)
  prast**ee**t-ye!
exhibition v**i**stafka
exit v**i**khat
expensive darag**oy**
explain abyeesn**ya**t'
eye drops glazn**i**ye k**a**plee
eyes glaz**a**

fabric tkan'
face leets**o**
fact fakt
faint *(unclear)* t**oo**skli
  (verb) tyer**ya**t'
  sazn**a**neeye
fair *(funfair)* **ya**rmarka
  (just) spravyedl**ee**vi
fall *(verb)* p**a**dat'
false teeth prat**ye**z
family syem'**ya**
fan *(ventilator)* vyenteel**ya**tar
  (enthusiast) bal**ye**l'shsheek
far dal**ye**ko
fare st**o**-eemast' pra**ye**zda
farm f**ye**rma
farmer f**ye**rmyer
fashion m**o**da

fast b**i**stro
fat *(person)* t**o**lsti
  (on meat etc) zheer
father at**ye**ts
fax machine faks
feel *(touch)* ch**oo**stvavat'
  I feel hot mnye zh**a**rka
  I don't feel well
  mnye pl**o**kha
feet n**o**gee
felt-tip pen flam**,a**styer
female zh**e**nskee
ferry par**o**m
fever leekhar**a**tka
few ny**e**skal'ka
fiancé zhen**ee**kh
fiancée nyev**ye**sta
field p**o**l-ye
fill in zapaln**ya**t'
filling *(tooth)* pl**o**mba
fill up napoln**ya**t'
film *(cinema)* feel'm
  (camera) pl**yo**nka
filter feeltr
find *(verb)* nakhad**ee**t'
finger p**a**lyets
Finland feenl**ya**ndee-ya
fire *(blaze)* pazh**a**r
fire exit pazh**a**rni v**i**khat
fire extinguisher agnyet**oo**sh**ee**tyel'
firework sal**yoo**t
first py**e**rvi
first aid sk**o**ra-ya p**o**mash'
first floor ftar**oy** et**a**sh
first name **ee**mya
fish r**i**ba
fishing r**i**bna-ya l**o**vlya
  to go fishing khad**ee**t' na rib**a**lkoo
fishing rod **oo**dachka
fishmonger r**i**bni magaz**ee**n
fizzy sheep**oo**chee
flag flak
flash *(camera)* fsp**i**shka

flat (*level*) ploskee
   (*apartment*) kvarteera
flavour fkoos
flea blakha
flight ryays
floor (*of building*) etash
   (*of room*) pol
flour mooka
flower tsvyetok
flu greep
flute flyayta
fly (*verb*) lyetyet'
   (*insect*) mookha
fog tooman
folk music narodna-ya moozika
food yeda
food poisoning peeshshevo-ye
   atravlyeneeye
foot naga
   on foot pyeshkom
football footbol
   (*ball*) footbol'ni myach
for dlya
   for me dlya myenya
   what for? dlya chyevo?
forbid zapryeshat'
foreigner (*man*)
   eenostranyets
   (*woman*) eenostranka
forest lyes
fork veelka
fortnight dvye nyedyelee
fountain pen aftaroochka
fourth chyetvyorti
fracture pyeryelom
free svabodni
   (*no cost*) byesplatni
freezer marazeel'neek
French frantsoozskee
fridge khaladeel'neek
friend (*male*) drook
   (*female*) padrooga
friendly droozheskee

from ot
   I'm from London ya eez londana
front: in front of pyeryet
frost maros
frozen (*adj; food*) zamarozheni
fruit frookt
fruit juice frooktovi sok
fry zhareet'
frying pan skavarada
full polni
   I'm full (*male*) ya sit
   (*female*) ya sita
funny (*amusing*) smyeshnoy
   (*odd*) strani
fur myekh
fur hat myekhava-ya
   shapka
furniture myebel'

game eegra
garage (*service station*) stantsee-ya
   tyekh-absloozheevanee-ya
   (*petrol station*) byenzakalonka
   (*parking*) garazh
garden sat
garlic chyesnok
gay (*homosexual*) galooboy
gear pyeryedacha
Georgia groozee-ya
German nyemyetskee
get (*fetch*) dastavat'
   have you got ...? oo vas yest' ...?
   to get the train oospyet' na po-yest
get back (*return*)
   vazvrashshat'sa
get in/on (*to transport*) sadeet'sa
get out vikhadeet'
get up (*rise*) fstavat'
gift padarak
gin dzheen
girl dyevooshka
girlfriend padrooga

give davat'
glad rat
  I'm glad (male) ya rat
  (female) ya rada
glasnost glasnast'
glass (for drinking) stakan
  (material) styeklo
glasses achkee
gloves pyerchatkee
glue klay
goggles zasheetniye achkee
gold zolata
good kharoshee
  good! kharasho
goodbye dasveedanee-ya
government praveetyel'stva
granddaughter vnoochka
grandfather dyedooshka
grandmother babooshka
grandson vnook
grapes veenagrat
grass trava
Great Britain
  vyeleekabreetanee-ya
green zyelyoni
grey syeri
grill greel'
grocer (shop) bakalyeya
ground floor pyervi etash
guarantee (noun) garantee-ya
  (verb) garanteeravat'
guard storash
guest gost'
guide book pootyevadeetyel'
guitar geetara
gun (rifle) roozh'yo

hair volasi
haircut streeshka
hairdresser pareekmakhyer
hair dryer fyen
hair spray lak dlya valos

half palaveena
  half an hour polchasa
ham vyetcheena
hammer malatok
hand rooka
handbag damska-ya soomka
handkerchief nasavoy platok
handle (door) roochka
handsome kraseevi
hangover pakhmyel'ye
happy shasleevi
harbour gavan'
hard tvyordi
  (difficult) tyazhyoli
hat shlyapa
have eemyet'
  I don't have ...
  oo myenya nyet ...
  have you got ...?
  oo vas yest' ...?
  I have to go now
  mnye para
hay fever syena-ya leekharatka
he on
head galava
headache galavna-ya bol'
health zdarov'ye
hear slishat'
hearing aid slookhavoy apparat
heart syerts-ye
heart attack syerdyechni preestoop
heating ataplyeneeye
heavy tyazhyoli
heel (foot) pyatka
  (shoe) kablook
hello zdrastvooyt-ye
help (noun) pomashsh'
  (verb) pamagat'
  help! pamageet-ye!
hepatitis gyepateet
her it's her eta ana
  for her dlya nyeyo
  give it to her atdlt-ye yay

her: her bag/bags yeyo soomka/soomkee
  her house yeyo dom
  her shoes yeyo tooflee
  it's hers eta yeyo
high visokee
hill kholm
him: it's him eta on
  for him dlya nyevo
  give it to him atdlt-ye yemoo
hire prakat
his: his book/books yevo kneega/
  kneegee
  his house yevo dom
  it's his eta yevo
history eestoree-ya
hitchhike pootyeshestvavat' afta-stopam
HIV positive veech-eenfeetsiravaniy
hobby khobee
holiday otpoosk
home dom
  at home doma
homeopathy gamyeapateeya
honest chyesni
honey myot
honeymoon myedovi myesyats
hope (verb) nadyeyat'sa
  (noun) nadyezhda
horn (car) seegnal
  (animal) rok
horrible oozhasni
horse loshat'
hospital bal'neetsa
hot water bottle gryelka
hour chas
house dom
how? kak?
  how much? skol'ka?
Hungary vyengree-ya
hungry: I'm hungry (male) ya galodyen
  (female) ya galodna
hurry: I'm in a hurry ya spyeshoo
hurt (verb) balyet'
husband moosh

I ya
ice lyot
ice cream marozhena-ye
ice hockey khakyay
ice lolly frooktova-ye marozhena-ye
ice skates kan'kee
ice skating katat'sa na kan'kakh
icicle sasool'ka
icon eekona
if yeslee
ill (male) bal'noy
  (female) bal'na-ya
illness balyezn'
immediately nyemyedlyena
important vazhni
impossible nyevazmozhna
in v
  in English pa-angleeskee
  in the hotel v gasteeneets-ye
Indian eendeeskee
indicator ookazatyel' pavarota
indigestion nyesvaryeneeye zhelootka
inhaler (for asthma etc) eengalyatar
infection eenfyektsee-ya
information eenfarmatsee-ya
information office
  spravachna-ye byooro
injection eenyektsee-ya
injury rana
ink chyerneela
insect nasyekoma-ye
insect repellent sryedstva ot
  nasyekomikh
insomnia byesoneetsa
insurance strakhofka
interesting eentyeryesni
international myezhdoo-narodni
internet eenternet
interpret pyeryevadeet'
interpreter pyeryevotcheek
into v
invitation preeglasheneeye
Ireland eerlandee-ya

113

Irish eerl*a*ntskee

Irishman eerl*a*ndets

Irishwoman eerl*a*ndka

iron (*metal*) zhel*ye*za

  (*for clothes*) oot*yoo*k

Iron Curtain zhel*ye*zni z*a*navyes

island *o*straf

it *e*ta

itch (*noun*) chyes*o*tka

  it itches

  chy*e*shetsa

jacket peedzh*a*k

jam var*ye*n'ye

jazz dzhas

jealous ryevn*ee*vi

jeans dzh*ee*nsi

jellyfish myed*oo*za

jeweller yoovyel*ee*r

job rab*o*ta

jog (*verb*) by*e*gat' troosts*oy*

joke sh*oo*tka

journey pay*e*stka

jump (*verb*) prig*a*t'

jumper dzh*e*mpyer

just t*ol*'ka/t*ol*'ka shto

key kly*oo*ch

KGB ka-ge-be

kidney p*o*chka

kilo keel*o*

kilometre keelam*ye*tr

kind d*o*bri

kitchen k*oo*khnya

knee kal*ye*na

knife nosh

knit vyaz*a*t'

know: I don't know

  ya nye zn*a*-yoo

Kremlin kry*e*ml'

label eteek*ye*tka

lace kr*oo*zheva

laces (*of shoe*) shnoork*ee*

lake *o*zyera

lamb (*meat*) bar*a*neena

lamp l*a*mpa

lampshade abazh*oo*r

land (*noun*) zyeml*ya*

  (*verb*) preezyeml*ya*t'sa

language yaz*i*k

large bal'sh*oy*

last (*final*) pasl*ye*dnee

  last week na pr*o*shlay nyed*ye*l-ye

  last month fpr*o*shlam m*ye*syats-ye

  at last! nakan*ye*ts

late: it's getting late p*o*zna

  the bus is late aft*o*boos ap*a*zdiva-yet

laugh smy*e*y*a*t'sa

launderette pr*a*chyechna-ya

  sama-absl*oo*zheevaneeye

laundry (*place*)

  pr*a*chyechna-ya

  (*dirty clothes*) gr*ya*zna-ye

  byel'*yo*

lavatory too-al*ye*t

laxative slab*ee*tyel'na-ye

lazy lyen*ee*vi

leaf leest

leaflet leest*o*fka

learn (*language*) eez*oo*chat'

leather k*o*zha

leave (*something somewhere*) ast*a*vlyat'

  (*by transport*) oo-ye-zh*a*t'

  (*on foot*) ookhad*ee*t'

left (*not right*) l*ye*vi

  there's nothing left

  neechy*e*vo nye ast*a*las'

left luggage (*locker*)

  k*a*myera khran*ye*nee-ya

leg nag*a*

lemon leem*o*n

lemonade leeman*a*t

length dlee*n*a

Lenin Library beeblee-atyeka
  eemyenee lyeneena
Lenin's Mausoleum mavzalyay
  lyeneena
lens leenza
less myen'she
lesson oorok
letter pees'mo
letter box pachtovi yasheek
lettuce list'ya salat
library beeblee-atyeka
licence vadeetyel'skeeye prava
life zheezn'
lift (in building) leeft
light (not heavy) lyokhkee
  (not dark) svyetli
lighter zazheegalka
lighter fuel byenzeen dlya zazheegalkee
like: I like you ti mnye nraveesh'sa
  I like swimming
  mnye nraveetsa plavat'
  it's like ... eta kak ...
lip gooba
lipstick goobna-ya pamada
liqueur leekyor
list speesak
listen slooshat'
Lithuania leetva
litre leetr
litter moosar
little (small) malyen'kee
  a little nyemnoga
liver pyechyen'
lollipop lyedyenyets
long dleeni
look at smatryet'
look for eeskat'
lorry groozaveek
lose tyeryat'
lost property byooro nakhodak
lot: a lot mnoga
loud gromkee
lounge gasteena-ya

love (noun) lyoobof'
  (verb) lyoobeet'
low neezkee
luck oodacha
  good luck! zhela-yoo oodachee!
luggage bagash
luggage rack bagazhna-ya polka
lunch abyet

magazine zhoornal
mail pochta
make dyelat'
make-up greem
male moozhskoy
man moozhcheena
manager admeeneestrator
many mnoga
map karta
  a map of Moscow karta maskvi
marble mramar
margarine margareen
market rinak
married (male) zhenat
  (female) zamoozhem
mascara toosh' dlya ryesneets
mass (church) myesa
match (light) speechka
  (sport) match
material (cloth) tkan'
mattress matras
maybe mozhet' bit'
me: it's me eta ya
  for me dlya myenya
  give it to me dat-ye mnye
meal yeda
meat myasa
mechanic myekhaneek
medicine lyekarstva
meet fstryechat'
meeting fstryecha
melon dinya
mens (toilet) moozhskoy too-alyet

menu myenyoo
message sa-abshshyeneeye
midday poldyen'
middle: in the middle
  pasyeryedeen-ye
midnight polnach'
milk malako
mine: it's mine eta moy
mineral water meenyeral'na-ya vada
minute meenoota
mirror zyerkala
Miss mees
miss (verb: train etc) apazdat'
mistake asheepka
  to make a mistake
  asheebat'sa
mobile phone mobeel'niy tyelyefon
modem madem
monastery manastir'
money dyen'gee
month myesyats
monument pamyatneek
moon loona
more bol'she
morning ootra
  in the morning ootram
mosaic mazayka
Moscow maskva
mosquito kamar
mother mat'
motorbike matatseekl
motorway afta-strada
mountain gara
mouse mish'
moustache oosi
mouth rot
move dveegat'sa
  don't move!
  nye dveegltyes'!
  (house) pyerye-yezhat'
movie feel'm
Mr gaspadeen
Mrs gaspazha

much mnoga
  not much nyemnoga
  much better/slower
  garazda looch-ye/myedlyenye-ye
mug krooshka
mum mama
museum moozyay
mushroom greep
music moozika
musical instrument
  moozikal'ni eenstroomyent
musician moozikant
mussels meedee
must dolzhen
mustard garcheetsa
my: my house moy dom
  my bag ma-ya soomka
  my keys ma-ee klyoochee

nail (metal) gvozd'
  (finger) nogat'
nailfile peelka dlya
  nagtyay
nail polish lak dlya nagtyay
name (first) eemya
  (last) fameelee-ya
nappy pyelyonka
narrow oozkee
near: near the door okala dvyeree
  near London okala Londana
necessary noozhni
neck sheya
necklace azheryel'ye
need (verb) noozhdat'sa
  I need ... mnye noozhna ...
  there's no need eta nyenoozhna
needle eegla
negative (photo) nyegateef
nephew plyemyaneek
never neekagda
new novi
news novastee

newsagent gaz<u>ye</u>tni kee-<u>o</u>sk
newspaper gaz<u>ye</u>ta
New Zealand n<u>o</u>va-ya zyel<u>a</u>ndee-ya
New Zealander (*man*)
  navazyel<u>a</u>ndyets
  (*woman*) navazyel<u>a</u>ntka
next sl<u>ye</u>dooyooshee
  next week na sl<u>ye</u>dooyooshshay
  nyed<u>ye</u>l-ye
  next month fsl<u>ye</u>dooyooshshem
  my<u>e</u>syatse
  what next? shto d<u>a</u>l'she?
nice pree<u>ya</u>tni
niece plyem<u>ya</u>neetsa
night noch'
nightclub nachn<u>oy</u> kloop
nightdress nachn<u>a</u>-ya
  roob<u>a</u>shka
  night porter nachn<u>oy</u> dyezh<u>oo</u>rni
no (*response*) nyet
  I have no money
  oo myen<u>ya</u> nyet d<u>ye</u>nyek
noisy sh<u>oo</u>mni
normal ab<u>i</u>chni
north s<u>ye</u>vyer
Northern Ireland
  s<u>ye</u>vyerna-ya eerl<u>a</u>ndee-ya
nose nos
not nye
notebook zapeesn<u>a</u>-ya kn<u>ee</u>shka
notice ab-yavly<u>e</u>neeye
novel ram<u>a</u>n
now tyep<u>ye</u>r'
nowhere neegd-<u>ye</u>
number n<u>o</u>myer
nurse myedsyestr<u>a</u>
nut (*fruit*) ar<u>ye</u>kh

occasionally eenagd<u>a</u>
occupation praf<u>ye</u>see-ya
occupied z<u>a</u>nyat

ocean akye-<u>a</u>n
October Revolution akty<u>e</u>br'ska-ya
  ryeval<u>yoo</u>tsee-ya
office <u>o</u>fees
often ch<u>a</u>sta
oil m<u>a</u>sla
ointment maz'
OK l<u>a</u>dna
old st<u>a</u>ri
olive masl<u>ee</u>na
omelette aml<u>ye</u>t
on na
one ad<u>ee</u>n
onion look
only t<u>o</u>l'ka
open (*verb*) atkriv<u>a</u>t'
  (*adj*) atkr<u>i</u>ti
opera <u>o</u>pyera
opposite: opposite the hotel
  napr<u>o</u>teef gast<u>ee</u>neetsi
optician <u>o</u>pteeka
or <u>ee</u>lee
orange (*colour*) ar<u>a</u>nzhevi
  (*fruit*) apyel's<u>ee</u>n
orange juice apyel's<u>ee</u>navi sok
orchestra arky<u>e</u>str
order (*in restaurant*)
  zak<u>a</u>zivat'
  out of order nye fpar<u>ya</u>tk-ye
ordinary (*normal*) ab<u>i</u>chni
other droog<u>oy</u>
  it's ours <u>e</u>ta n<u>a</u>she
out: he's out yev<u>o</u> nyet
outside na <u>oo</u>leets-ye
over nad
  over there tam
overtake abgan<u>ya</u>t'

pack of cards kal<u>o</u>da kart
package pak<u>ye</u>t
  (*parcel*) pas<u>i</u>lka

packet pachka
page straneetsa
pain bol'
paint *(noun)* kraska
painting karteena
pair para
Pakistani pakeestanskee
palace dvaryets
pale blyedni
pancakes bleeni
paper boomaga
parcel pasilka
pardon? prasteet-ye?
parents radeetyelee
park *(noun)* park
    (verb) staveet' masheenoo
part chast'
party *(celebration)* vyechyereenka
    (political) partee-ya
Party member chlyen partee
passenger pasazheer
passport pasport
path trapeenka
pavement tratoo-ar
pay plateet'
peace meer
peach pyerseek
peanuts arakhees
pear groosha
pearl zhemchook
peas garokh
pedestrian pyeshekhot
pen roochka
pencil karandash
penknife pyeracheeni nosh
pensioner pyensee-anyer
people lyoodee
people's narodni
pepper pyeryets
per: per night zanach'
perestroika pyeryestroyka
perfect pryevaskhodni
perfume dookhee

perhaps mozhet bit'
perm zaveefka pyermanyent
permission razryesheneeye
petrol byenzeen
phonecard tyelyefonaya kartachka
photocopier ksyeraks
photograph *(noun)* fatagrafee-ya
    (verb) fatagrafeeravat'
photographer fatograf
phrase book razgavorneek
piano fartyep'yana
picnic peekneek
piece koosok
pillow padooshka
pilot peelot
pin boolafka
pine *(tree)* sasna
pineapple ananas
ping-pong peeng-pong
pink rozavi
pipe *(for smoking)* troopka
    (for water) troobaprovat
pizza peetsa
place myesta
plain prastoy
plant rastyeneeye
plaster *(for cut)* plastir'
plastic plasteekavi
plastic bag plasteekavi pakyet
plate taryelka
platform platforma
play *(noun: theatre)* p'yesa
    (verb) eegrat'
please pazhalsta
plug *(electrical)*
    shtyepsyel'
    (sink) propka
plum sleeva
pocket karman
poison atravlyeneeye
Poland pol'sha
police meeleetsee-ya
police officer meeleetsee-anyer

police station atdyel<u>ye</u>neeye meel<u>ee</u>tsee-ya
politics pal<u>ee</u>teeka
pollution zagryazn<u>ye</u>neeye
poor by<u>e</u>dni
  (bad quality) plakh<u>oy</u>
pop music pop m<u>oo</u>zika
popular papool<u>ya</u>rni
pork sveen<u>ee</u>na
port (harbour) port
porter (for luggage) nas<u>ee</u>l'shsheek
possible vazm<u>o</u>zhni
post (noun) p<u>o</u>chta
  (verb) pasil<u>at</u>'
postbox pacht<u>o</u>vi <u>ya</u>shsheek
postcard atkr<u>i</u>tka
poster plak<u>at</u>
post office p<u>o</u>chta
postman pachtal'<u>o</u>n
potato kart<u>o</u>fyel'
poultry pt<u>ee</u>tsa
pound foont
powder (washing) parash<u>o</u>k
  (talcum) p<u>oo</u>dra
pram dy<u>e</u>tska-ya kal<u>ya</u>ska
prawn kryev<u>ye</u>tka
pregnant byer<u>ye</u>myena-ya
prescription ryets<u>ye</u>pt
present pad<u>a</u>rak
pretty kras<u>ee</u>vi
price tsyen<u>a</u>
priest svyashsh<u>ye</u>neek
private ch<u>a</u>sni
problem prabl<u>ye</u>ma
profession praf<u>ye</u>see-ya
public abshsh<u>ye</u>stvyeni
pull tyan<u>oo</u>t'
puncture prak<u>o</u>l
pure ch<u>ee</u>sti
purple fee-al<u>ye</u>tavi
purse kashel<u>yo</u>k
push tolk<u>at</u>'
put klast'
pyjamas peezh<u>a</u>ma

quality k<u>a</u>chyestva
quantity kal<u>ee</u>chyestva
quay pr<u>ee</u>chal
question vapr<u>o</u>s
queue (noun) <u>o</u>chyeryet'
  (verb) stay<u>at</u>' v<u>o</u>chyeryedee
quick b<u>i</u>stri
quiet t<u>ee</u>khee
quite (fairly) dav<u>o</u>l'na
  (fully) safs<u>ye</u>m

radiator batar<u>ye</u>ya
radio r<u>a</u>dee-o
radish ryed<u>ee</u>ska
railway line
  zhelyezna-dar<u>o</u>zhna-ya l<u>ee</u>nee-ya
rain dosht'
raincoat plashsh'
raisins eez<u>yoo</u>m
rare (uncommon) ry<u>e</u>tkee
  (steak) skr<u>o</u>v'yoo
rat kr<u>i</u>sa
razor br<u>ee</u>tva
razor blades
  br<u>ee</u>tvyeniye ly<u>e</u>zvee-ya
read cheet<u>at</u>'
ready gat<u>o</u>f
real nastay<u>a</u>shshee
rear lights z<u>a</u>dneeye f<u>a</u>ri
receipt chyek
receive pal<u>oo</u>chat'
receptionist receptionist
recommend ryekamy<u>e</u>ndavat'
record (music) plast<u>ee</u>nka
  (sporting etc) ry<u>e</u>kort
record player pra-<u>ee</u>grivatyel'
red kr<u>a</u>sni
Red Army kr<u>a</u>sna-ya arm<u>ee</u>ya
Red Square kr<u>a</u>sna-ya pl<u>o</u>shshat'
relative r<u>o</u>dstvyeneek
relax atdikh<u>at</u>'
religion ryel<u>ee</u>gee-ya

remember pomneet'
  I don't remember ya nye pomnyoo
rent (*verb*) naneemat'
reservation zakas
reserve zakazivat'
rest (*remainder*) astatak
  (*relax*) otdikh
restaurant ryestaran
return (*come back*) vazvrashshat'sa
  (*give back*) vazvrashshat'
return ticket abratni beelyet
rice rees
rich bagati
right (*correct*) praveel'ni
  (*direction*) pravi
  on the right naprava
ring (*telephone*) zvaneet'
  (*wedding etc*) kal'tso
ripe zryeli
river ryeka
road daroga
rock (*stone*) skala
  (*music*) rok
roll (*bread*) boolachka
Romania roomeenee-ya
roof krisha
room komnata
  (*in hotel*) nomyer
  (*space*) myesta
rope vyeryofka
rose roza
round (*circular*) kroogli
  it's my round moy chyeryot
rowing boat vyosyel'na-ya lotka
rubber (*eraser*) ryezeenka
  (*material*) ryezeena
rubbish moosar
ruby (*stone*) roobeen
rucksack ryookzak
rug (*mat*) kovreek
  (*blanket*) adyeyala
ruins roo-eeni
ruler (*for drawing*) leenyayka

rum rom
run (*person*) byezhat'
Russia rasee-ya
Russian (*adj*) rooskee
  (*man*) rooskee
  (*woman*) rooska-ya
Russian Orthodox Church
  rooska-ya pravaslavna-ya tserkaf'

sad groosni
safe byezapasni
safety pin angleeska-ya
  boolafka
salad salat
salami kapchyona-ya
  kalbasa
sale (*at reduced prices*)
  raspradazha
salesperson pradavyets
salmon lasos'
salt sol'
same: the same dress to zhe plat'ye
  the same people
  tye zhe lyoodee
samovar samavar
sand pyesok
sandals sandalee
sandwich bootyerbrot
sanitary towels
  geegee-yeneechyeskeeye salfyetkee
satellite TV
  spootneekavaye tyelyeveedeeneeye
sauce so-oos
saucepan kastryoolya
saucer blyoots-ye
sauna sa-oona
sausage saseeska
say gavareet'
  what did you say?
  shto vi skazalee?
  how do you say ...?
  kak boodyet ...?

scarf sharf
  (head) platok
scent dookhee
school shkola
scissors nozhneetsi
score shshyot
Scotland shatlandee-ya
Scotsman shatlandyets
Scotswoman shatlantka
Scottish shatlantskee
screw veent
screwdriver atvyortka
sculpture skool'ptoora
sea mor-ye
seafood marskeeye pradookti
seat myesta
second syekoonda
  (in series) ftaroy
see veedyet'
  I can't see
   ya nye veezhoo
  I see! paneemayoo!
seem kazat'sa
sell pradavat'
sellotape® leepkaya lyenta
send pasilat'
separate atdyel'ni
serious syer'yozni
serve absloozheevat'
service *(restaurant)*
  absloozheevaneeye
  (church) sloozhba
serviette salfyetka
several nyeskal'ka
sew sheet'
shade tyen'
shallow myelkee
shampoo shampoon'
shape forma
sharp ostri
shave *(noun)* breet'yo
  (verb) breet'sa
shaving foam kryem dlya breet'ya

shawl shal'
she ana
sheet prastinya
sherry khyeryes
ship parakhot
shirt roobashka
shoelaces shnoorkee
shoe polish kryem dlya oboovee
shoes tooflee
shop magazeen
shore byerek
short karotkee
shorts shorti
shoulder plyecho
show pakazivat'
shower *(bath)* doosh
shower gel gyel' dlyadoosha
shrimp kryevyetka
shut *(verb)* zakrivat'
Siberia seebeer
sick *(ill)* bal'noy
  I feel sick
   ya plokha syebya choostvoo-yoo
side *(edge)* starana
sidelights padfarneekee
sights: the sights of …
  dasta-preemyechatyel'nastee …
sign znak
silk shyolk
silver *(metal)* syeryebro
simple prastoy
sing pyet'
single *(one)* adeen
  (unmarried: man) khalastoy
  (woman) nyezamoozhnya-ya
single room adnamyesni nomyer
sister syestra
sit down sadeet'sa
size razmyer
ski *(verb)* katat'sa na lizhakh
skid *(verb)* zanaseet'
skirt yoopka
skis lizhee

sky nyeba

sleep (*noun*) son
   (*verb*) spat'
  to go to bed lazheet'sa spat'
sleeping bag spal'ni myeshok
sleeping car spal'ni vagon
sleeping pill snatvorna-ye
slippers tapachkee
slow myedlyeni
small malyen'kee
smell (*noun*) zapakh
   (*verb*) pakhnoot'
smile (*noun*) oolipka
   (*verb*) oolibat'sa
smoke (*noun*) dim
   (*verb*) kooreet'
snack zakooska
snow snyek
  it's snowing
  eedyot snyek
snow plough
  snyega-ooborachna-ya masheena
snowstorm snyezhna-ya boorya
so: so good tak kharasho
soap milo
socialism satsee-aleezm
socks naskee
soda water gazeerovana-ya vada
somebody kto-ta
somehow kak-ta
something shto-ta
sometimes eenagda
somewhere gdye-ta
son sin
song pyesnya
sorry! eezveeneet-ye!
  I'm sorry
  eezveeneet-ye
soup soop
south yook
souvenir soovyeneer
Soviet savyetskee
Soviet Union savyetskee sayoos

spade (*shovel*) lapata
spanner gayechni klyooch
spark plug zapal'na-ya svyecha
speak gavareet'
  do you speak ...?
  vi gavareet-ye pa-...?
  I don't speak ...
  ya nye gavaryoo pa- ...
spectacles achkee
spend (*money*) trateet'
   (*time*) pravadeet'
spider pa-ook
spinach shpeenat
spine speena
spoon loshka
sport sport
sprain rastyazheneeye
spring (*mechanical*) ryesora
spy shpee-on
square (*town*) ploshshat'
stadium stadee-on
stage stsyena
stairs lyesneetsa
stalls (*theatre*) parter
stamp marka
stand (*verb*) stayat'
star zvyezda
   (*film*) keenazvyezda
start (*verb*) nacheenat'
station (*mainline terminal*) vagzal
   (*underground*) stantsee-ya
statue statoo-ya
stay (*verb*) astanavleevat'sa
steak beefshtyeks
steal krast'
  it's been stolen ookralee
Steppes styep'
sting (*noun*) ookoos
   (*verb*) koosat'
  it stings zhot'
stockings choolkee
stomach zheloodak
stomachache bol'vzhelootk-ye

stop (*something*) astan<u>a</u>vleevat'
  (*come to a halt*) astan<u>a</u>vleevat'sa
  (*bus stop*) astan<u>o</u>fka
  stop! stoy!
storm b<u>oo</u>rya
strawberry kloobn<u>ee</u>ka
stream (*small river*) roochy<u>ay</u>
street <u>oo</u>leetsa
string (*cord*) vyery<u>o</u>fka
  (*guitar etc*) stroon<u>a</u>
student (*male*) stoody<u>e</u>nt
  (*female*) stoody<u>e</u>ntka
stupid gl<u>oo</u>pi
suburbs pr<u>ee</u>garat
suddenly vdr<u>oo</u>k
sugar s<u>a</u>khar
suit (*noun*) kasty<u>oo</u>m
  (*verb*) eet<u>ee</u>
  it suits you vam eed<u>yo</u>t
suitcase chyemad<u>a</u>n
sun s<u>o</u>ntse
sunbathe zagar<u>a</u>t'
sunburn s<u>o</u>lnyechni azh<u>o</u>k
sunglasses s<u>o</u>lnyechniye achk<u>ee</u>
sunny: it's sunny s<u>o</u>lnyechna
suntan zag<u>a</u>r
suntan lotion m<u>a</u>sla dlya zag<u>a</u>ra
supermarket ooneevyers<u>a</u>m
supper <u>oo</u>zheen
supplement dapaln<u>ye</u>neeye
sure oovy<u>e</u>ryeni
  are you sure?
  vi oovy<u>e</u>ryeni
surname fam<u>ee</u>lee-ya
surprise (*verb*) oodeevl<u>ya</u>t'
sweat (*noun*) pot
  (*verb*) paty<u>e</u>t'
sweet (*not sour*) sl<u>a</u>tkee
  (*candy*) kanfy<u>e</u>tka
swim pl<u>a</u>vat'
swimming cap koopal'na-ya sh<u>a</u>pachka
swimming costume koop<u>a</u>l'ni kasty<u>oo</u>m
swimming pool basy<u>ay</u>n

swimming trunks pl<u>a</u>fkee
switch viklyoochatyel'
synagogue seenag<u>o</u>ga

table stol
tablet tabl<u>ye</u>tka
take brat'
take off (*noun*) atpravl<u>ye</u>neeye
talcum powder tal'k
talk (*noun*) razgav<u>o</u>r
  (*verb*) razgav<u>a</u>reevat'
tall vis<u>o</u>kee
tampon tamp<u>o</u>n
tap kran
taste fk<u>oo</u>s
tea chI
tea towel pas<u>oo</u>dna-ye palaty<u>e</u>ntse
team kam<u>a</u>nda
telegram tyelyegr<u>a</u>ma
telephone (*noun*) tyelyef<u>o</u>n
  (*verb*) zvan<u>ee</u>t'
telephone box tyelyef<u>o</u>n-aftam<u>a</u>t
telephone call tyelyef<u>o</u>ni zvan<u>o</u>k
television tyelyev<u>ee</u>zar
temperature tyempyerat<u>oo</u>ra
tennis t<u>ye</u>nees
tent palatk<u>a</u>than chyem
thank (*verb*) blagadar<u>ee</u>t'
  thanks, thank you spas<u>ee</u>ba
that: that bus tot aft<u>o</u>boos
  that woman ta zh<u>e</u>nshsheena
  what's that? shto <u>e</u>ta?
  I think that …
  ya d<u>oo</u>ma-yoo shto …
theatre ty<u>ea</u>tr
their: their room
  eekh k<u>o</u>mnata
  it's theirs <u>e</u>ta eekh
them: it's them <u>e</u>ta an<u>ee</u>
  for them dlya n<u>ee</u>kh
  give it to them atd<u>I</u>t-ye eem
then tagd<u>a</u>

123

there tam
  there is/are …
  eemye-yetsa/eemye-yootsa..
  is/are there …? zdyes' est' …?
  is there a bank here?
  zdyes' yest' bank?
thermometer gradoosneek
thermos flask tyermas
these: these things etee vyeshshee
  these are mine eta ma-ee
they anee
thick (wide) tolsti
thief vor
thin tonkee
thing vyeshsh'
think doomat'
  I think so ya dooma-yoo shto da
  I'll think about it
  yapadooma-yoo ab etam
third trye'tee
thirsty: I'm thirsty ya
  khachoo peet'
this: this bus etat
  aftoboos
  this woman eta
  zhenshsheena
  what's this? shto eta?
  this is Mr …. eta gaspadeen …
those: those things tye vyeshshee
  those are his eta yevo
throat gorla
throat pastilles tablyetkee at kashlya
through chyeryes
thunderstorm graza
ticket beelyet
ticket office beelyetna-ya kasa
tie (noun) galstook
  (verb) zavyazivat'
tights kalgotkee
time vryemya
  what's the time? katori chas?
timetable raspeesaneeye
tin kansyervna-ya banka

tin opener kansyervni nosh
tip (money) cha-yeviye
tired oostali
  I'm tired (male) ya oostal
  (female) ya oostala
tissues boomazhniye salfyetkee
to: to England vanglee-yoo
  to the station na vagzal
  to the doctor k vrachoo
toast padzharyeni khlyep
tobacco tabak
today syevodnya
together fmyest-ye
toilet too-alyet
toilet paper too-alyetna-ya boomaga
tomato pameedor
tomato juice tamatni sok
tomorrow zaftra
tongue yazik
tonic toneek
tonight syevodnya
  vyechyeram
too (also) tagzhe
  (excessive) sleeshkam
tooth zoop
toothache zoobna-ya bol'
toothbrush zoobna-ya
  shshyotka
toothpaste zoobna-ya pasta
torch fanareek
touch trogat'
tour ekskoorsee-ya
tourist tooreest
tourist office tooreesteechyeska-ye
  byooro
towel palatyentse
tower bashnya
town gorat
town hall ratoosha
toy eegrooshka
tracksuit tryeneerovachni kastyoom
tractor traktar
tradition tradeetsee-ya

traffic ooleechna-ye dveezh@neeye
traffic jam pr@pka
train p@-yest
tram tramvl
Trans-Siberian Express
  trans-seeb@erskee ekspr@s
translate pyeryevad@et'
travel pootyesh@stvavat'
travel agency byoor@
  pootyesh@stvee
traveller's cheque dar@zhni chyek
tray padn@s
tree dy@ryeva
trolleybus traly@yboos
trousers bry@okee
truth pr@vda
try (*experimentally*) pr@bavat'
  (*endeavour*) star@t'sa
tunnel toony@el'
Turkmenistan toorkmy@enee-ya
turn pavar@cheevat'
tweezers peents@et
typewriter p@eshooshsha-ya mash@enka

Ukraine ookra-@ena
umbrella z@onteek
uncle dy@dya
uncomfortable nye-ood@obni
under pod
underground myetr@
underpants troos@i
understand paneem@at'
  I don't understand ya nye paneema-yoo
underwear n@ezhnye-ye byel'y@o
United States sa-yedeeny@oniye sht@ti
university ooneevyerseet@yet
unmarried (*man*) nyezhen@at
  (*female*) nyez@amoozhem
until do
unusual nye-ab@ichni
upwards navy@erkh
upstairs navyerkh@oo

Urals oor@l
urgent sr@chni
us: it's us @eta mi
  it's for us @eta dlya nas
  give it to us d@lt-ye nam
use (*noun*) oopatryebl@yeneeye
  (*verb*) oopatryebl@yat'
  it's no use nye rab@ota-yet
useful paly@ezni
useless byespaly@ezni
USSR es-es-es-er
usual ab@ichni
usually ab@ichna

vacant (*room*) svab@odni
vacuum cleaner pilyes@os
valid dyaystv@eetyel'ni
valley dal@eena
valve kl@pan
vanilla van@eel'
vase v@za
veal tyely@teena
vegetable @ovashsh
vegetarian (*person*) vyegyetaree@anyets
very @ochyen'
vest m@lka
video tape v@edyeo-kas@yeta
view veet
villa v@ela
village dyer@yevnya
vinegar @ooksoos
violin skr@eepka
visa v@eeza
visit (*noun*) pasyeshshy@eneeye
  (*verb*) pasyeshsh@at'
visitor pasy@et@eetyel'
  (*tourist*) toor@eest
vitamin veetam@een
vodka v@tka
voice g@las
voltage napryazh@eneeye

125

wait zhdat'
waiter afeetsee-**ant**
  waiter! afeetsee-**ant!**
waiting room zal azheed**a**nee-ya
waitress afeetsee-**antka**
Wales oo**e**l's
walk (*noun: stroll*) prag**oo**lka
  (*verb*) g**oo**lyat'
  to go for a walk eet**ee** na prag**oo**lkoo
wall sty**e**n**a**
wallet boom**a**zhneek
want khat**y**et'
  I want … ya khach**oo** …
war vl**n**a
wardrobe shkaf
warm t**y**opli
was: I was (*male*) ya bil
  (*female*) ya bil**a**
  it was eta bil**a**
washing powder steer**a**l'ni parash**o**k
washing-up liquid
  zh**ee**dkast' dlya mit'**ya** pas**oo**di
wasp as**a**
watch (*noun*) chas**i**
  (*verb*) smatr**y**et'
water vad**a**
waterfall vadap**a**d
wave (*noun*) valn**a**
  (*verb*) makh**a**t'
we mi
weather pag**o**da
Web site vep-s**i**t
wedding sv**a**d'ba
week nyed**y**elya
welcome dabr**o** pazh**a**lavat'
  you're welcome pazh**a**lsta
wellingtons ryez**ee**naviye sapag**ee**
Welsh oo**e**l'skee
were: we were mi b**i**lee
  you were (*plural, formal*) vi b**i**lee
  (*singular, familiar*) (*male*) ti bil
  (*female*) ti bil**a**
  they were an**ee** b**i**lee

west z**a**pat
  in the West na z**a**pad-ye
wet m**o**kri
what? shto?
wheel kaly**e**s**o**
wheelchair eenval**ee**dna-ya kal**ya**ska
when? k**a**gda?
where? gdye?
which? kak**o**y?
while pak**a**
whisky v**ee**skee
white b**y**eli
who? kto?
whole ts**e**li
whose? chyay?
why? pachyem**oo**?
wide sheer**o**kee
wife zhen**a**
wild d**ee**kee
win vi**ee**grivat'
wind v**y**etyer
window akn**o**
wine veen**o**
wing kril**o**
wish zhel**a**t'
with s
without byez
woman zhenshsheena
women (*toilet*) zh**e**nskee too-al**y**et
wonderful chood**y**esni
wood d**y**eryeva
wool shyerst'
word sl**o**va
work (*noun*) rab**o**ta
  (*verb*) rab**o**tat'
worry (*verb*) val'n**a**vat'sa
worse kh**oo**zhe
worst kh**oo**dshee
wrapping paper aby**o**rtachna-ya
  boom**a**ga
wrist zap**ya**st'ye
writing paper pacht**o**va-ya boom**a**ga
wrong nyepr**a**veel'ni

year got
yellow zholti
yes da
yesterday fchyera
yet yeshshyo
   not yet yeshshyo nyet
you vi
   (singular familiar) ti
your vash
   (singular, familiar) tvoy
   your book vasha/tvaya kneega
   your shoes vashee/tva-ee tooflee
yours: is this yours? eta vashe?/tvayo?

zip molnee-ya
zoo zaapark